The Language of Trusted Leaders

Jack Ricchiuto

Books by Jack Ricchiuto

Collaborative Creativity / 1996
Accidental Conversations / 2002
Project Zen / 2003
Appreciative Leadership / 2005
Mountain Paths / 2007
Conscious Becoming / 2008
Instructions From The Cook / 2009
The Stories That Connect Us / 2010
Enchantment Of Casual Origins / 2011
The Joy Of Thriving / 2012
Ordinary Eyes / 2012
The Agile Canvas Field Guide / 2012
Abundant Possibilities / 2013
The Power Of Circles / 2013
Making Sense Of Time / 2014
Beyond Recipes / 2014
Focus / 2015
Smarter Together / 2015
Ideas / 2015
The Art Of Conversations / 2016
The Way Of Questions / 2017
The Growth Imperative / 2018
Simple Listening / 2019
Path / 2019
The Poetry of Human Emotion / 2020
A Radical Kindness / 2021
The Language of Trusted Leaders / 2021

The Language of Trusted Leaders

Jack Ricchiuto
Nuance Works
1020 Kenilworth Avenue
Cleveland OH 44113 USA

NuanceWorks.com

Copyright 2021 Jack Ricchiuto
All rights reserved.

ISBN 9798584407452

Paperback
I. Title
1. Leadership.

First edition, January 2021
Printed in the USA
Production: Kindle Direct Publishing
Cover: Tia Andrako

Contents

- 7. Invitation
- 11. Leadership
- 35. Language
- 81. Direction
- 95. Velocity
- 117. Generativity
- 133. Learning
- 157. Personas
- 181. Listening
- 192. Epilogue

Invitation

Over the past four decades, I have had the honor and delight to work with leaders across industries and professions. Across the US and globally I've worked with all levels of leaders in the public and private sectors.

I've trained them by the hundreds and coached them individually. I've seen more varieties of leaders than I could count. I've worked with leaders who were just brilliant and others who were just awful, according to people on their teams.

Assessing leadership competency is not complicated. We just look at how their people feel about them, their work, themselves, and each other.

We see how people on their teams do; we listen to how they sound; we notice how they interact with each other; we pay attention to what they take home with them. We observe how much they trust their leaders.

The invitation here is to explore and understand what distinguishes trusted leaders from others.

Is it their education, training, or pedigree? Is it their gender, generation, or geography? Is it their compensation or incentives? Is it what boxes they're assigned by personality tests?

It's been my experience that none of these directly determine who is and isn't a trusted leader.

The premise here is simple: the most salient defining factor in the character of leadership is the language leaders use in their everyday interactions with people.

It is the most significant takeaway from my first 42 years of doing leadership development work and writing.

This book is dedicated to new, emerging, and developing leaders. This includes people who are beginning to lead teams of leaders.

The approach to leadership here has been inspired by teachers Fernando Flores, Meg Wheatley, Peter Block, Brene Brown, David Rock, and Lisa Feldman Barrett.

You will discover over 300 examples of the kinds of language that engage people and teams to be their best selves in their work. It presents 32 principles trusted leaders use as a compass in navigating the varieties of situations and uncertainties they encounter.

It outlines the 8 language actions: declarations, commitments, timing, agreements, requests, assessments, offers, and acceptances.

It details language to use in supporting the 12 archetypal team members: The Struggling, Inconsolables, One Foot Out the Door, Eye on the Door, Entitled Class, Guardians of The Status Quo, Newbies, Careerists, Hyper-achievers, Soloists, Likables, and Entrepreneurs.

This is a companion guide to support the arc of your learning and life as a trusted leader.

Enjoy the journey.

Jack Ricchiuto
January 2021

Leadership

The trusted leader imperative

This is an era that calls for trusted leaders. We need them in companies and communities, in non-profits and networks, institutions and governments.

On every scale, our problems and opportunities are more varied and complex than ever. They span economic, social, technical, political, cultural, and spiritual domains. They require models of leadership distinct from the past. They require trusted leaders.

Trusted leaders work from a core focus: making it easier for people to be their best selves together.

Making things easier is at the heart of human-centered workplaces. It is, at last, optimally and ultimately respectful of the people who make organizations successful.

Trusted leaders know this. They don't suffer delusions of grandeur that they are the center of their universe or that their efforts count more than those they have the privilege to support. They are trusted for their humility, perspective, and passion for service to the success of others.

We don't have a leadership shortage. We have enough people in leadership positions. We need trusted leaders.

As you develop as a leader, you will have the opportunity to learn how to become a trusted leader. Your world will be better for it.

The character of trust

Trust is social capital. When others trust us as leaders, they are more likely to show up as their best selves, work well together, and continuously learn their way into the future. This is the power of trust.

Trust is grown and sustained through three characteristics: credibility, dependability, and likability.

We act with credibility when others are confident we will deliver what's true, accurate, and verifiable. They can count on us to make clear what we don't know. People can trust what we say.

We act with dependability when others know they can expect us to support their success and well-being. Their best is our North Star. They are not the tools of our success. People can trust what we do.

We act with likability when others know we have things in common with them: shared emotions, stories, qualities, values, likes, and dislikes. People trust people they like; people like people like themselves. People can trust who we are.

Trust is a continuum from distrust to trust. Distrust is expecting someone to be other than credible, dependable, or likable. Trust is feeling confident in expecting these from others.

Midway on the continuum is a lack of trust. Here, we are not distrustful nor are we strongly trustful. Trust simply hasn't yet been built. Trust is more potential than actual.

Trust is built one layer at a time through the shared language of conversations, actions, and experiences.

People perform, learn, and interact differently when they are supported by trusted leaders in contrast to when they report to leaders they distrust or don't yet trust.

The highest level of leadership competency is learning to be a trusted leader.

Teams of trusted leaders

When people are supported by trusted leaders a sense of trusting and trustworthiness is palpable and pervasive on the team.

People act in trusting and trustworthy ways with each other. People trust themselves. These create vital patterns and possibilities of courage and creativity that drives their growth and the team's growth in its contributions to the organization's growth.

As a result, the velocity and vibe of the team are vibrant. Velocity and vibe are the flow and feel of the team.

Trust is not one of those unseen indicators that require measurement tools to become knowable.

Trust is obvious to anyone on the team and who interacts with the team. No one has to go through a slide deck or spreadsheet report to know what they see, hear, and feel. If they don't see, hear, and feel trust, they don't need a report telling them.

As trusted leaders, we don't lecture people on how they need to trust us, each other, or themselves more. Trust cannot be commanded. It is built and deepened as we work together with everyday alignment, sync, and respect.

Because our work and personal lives are indivisibly interwoven, being trusting and trustworthy follows us home.

Trust is not mysterious or elusive. Being a trusted and trusting leader is about learning.

When leaders struggle with trust

It is common for high-performers on teams to be promoted to leadership positions.

Each brings with them a sense of what it means to be a leader. This sense has been shaped by parents, teachers, coaches, mentors, role models, and bosses.

Leaders struggle until they learn what trusted leadership is and how it works. As they struggle, their teams struggle.

There are two kinds of fortunate struggling leaders: the lucky and the learners.

The lucky inherit teams where peer trust is strong. Their teams do well regardless of the leadership that shows up or doesn't. These leaders are, as the saying goes, like someone who wakes up on third base and think they hit a triple.

The learners are fortunate enough to learn trusted leadership through whatever resources and opportunities are available. They learn to understand, appreciate, and practice the fine art and rigorous science of trusted leadership.

They struggle less. Their teams flourish more. Everyone notices and the beneficiaries are many.
The trusted leader manifesto

With an entrepreneurial mindset, trusted leaders work from a place of empathy. We are here to support, not to be served.

We know how challenging work can be. Demands exceed capacity and resources. Change and uncertainty are constants. As human beings, we are intrinsically gifted and imperfect. Change and uncertainty are constants favoring those who love new questions.

Empathy inspires our core commitment to make things easier for people. We use whatever talents, resources, and latitudes we have to daily fulfill this commitment.

We have no interest in worrying about control. It's too costly; it slows things down; it makes things harder. There is little empathy in that. It is disrespectful.

Our priority is making it easier for people to get things done together, learn together, and celebrate leaving the world better than they found it.

Our empathy and vision for this make us trusted leaders. We are regularly delighted but not surprised by the performance of our teams.

The power of language

As trusted leaders, we are known for the achievements of our teams.

People show up with honesty, curiosity, agility, alignment, and passion for learning. They show up in these ways because they feel they are genuinely invited, valued, respected, and supported by us and each other.

Teams with trusted leaders tend to be more caring, responsible, learning-driven, collaborative, coordinated, and proactive. Without trusted leaders teams tend to be more critical, defensive, risk-averse, divided, reactive, and overwhelmed.

People feel supported because they know we care how they feel.

A keen interest in how people feel is the cornerstone of empathy. We know at least intuitively what the latest brain science indicates: how we do is shaped by how we feel. Our emotions shape how we perform and interact. How we feel is shaped by language.

Before leaders learn how emotions work, they spend little time mindfully noticing and empathetically responding to people's emotions. They also have no idea how their language shapes how people feel, perform, and interact every day.

This further makes distrust and non-trust likely. People don't feel respected and it shows in their performance and interactions.

Trusted leaders stay intentional about how their language influences what people feel and do in their work. They know everything they say and ask is emotionally charged and trust shaping.

As a result, people trust their leaders, each other, and themselves. Language has this power.

Self-organizing teams

Teams work along a continuum between leader-dependent and self-organizing. The character of leadership makes a difference.

The more self-organizing a team, th more people share the responsibility to make sure work is coordinated, people are supported, learning happens, and an optimal emotional tone is sustained.

They do this with the support of shared tools and agreements. They take and share initiative instead of waiting for permission. Their leader is committed to making all of this easier.

The more leader-dependent a team, the less people feel free to take initiative and share responsibility for the work.

Their velocity is slower because they have to wait on their bottlenecked leaders for assignments, permissions, feedback, support, solutions, resources, and approvals.

To be clear, leaders of self-organizing teams have as much work to do as leaders of leader-dependent teams. It's just different work. It is also less stressful because it's work as a trusted leader.

Teams accustomed to being leader-dependent can, with trusted leaders, learn how to be more trusted self-organizing teams.

The language of permission

Much of our language as trusted leaders explicitly and implicitly help people work without the bottlenecks of our permissions.

Many people are accustomed to leaders who worry about control. They don't automatically know we want them to take initiative in ways they can.

We have to make this clear in our language with them until they get the message. In a sense, we give them promission: permission to not need permission.

We have confidence in people taking initiative because we make it easier for them to know what good and great look like and to learn how to perform and interact at these levels.

We want them to do what they can do, communicate what they can communicate, and learn what they can learn. They become unstoppable together. Who doesn't want that?

Trusted leadership principles

Part of what earns trust is working from principles. Principled leadership is trustworthy because we make it easier for people to know what to expect from us.

Principles are rules of thumb, guides to action. They reflect and inspire values. Using the language of principles makes transparent what's behind something we as a leader say, ask, and do.

Here are 32 principles of trusted leaders. They are organized into 5 themes: alignment, velocity, learning, change, and generativity.

They are described in the kinds of language we would use as leaders with our teams. As with all the suggested language throughout the book, you will make the language your own.

Alignment

Values are a compass in uncertainty and change

We need a compass to navigate the constancy of uncertainty and change. Our values are our compass. They are what's most important to us as we contribute our best to our world. With shared values, we navigate together in the same direction.

Dreams are lenses that reveal new opportunities in the present

Dreams are what want to see and make possible. Dreams reveal new possibilities unseen without dreams. They are lenses revealing new and available possibilities. We dream out as far into the future as we can. The farther out we go in time the larger our lens.

Alignment is trust; people move at the speed of trust

When we align on shared values, we work with trust in ourselves, each other, in our relationships, and the whole. Our velocity is a function of our trust. The greater the shared trust the greater our velocity. Trust accelerates empathy, learning, performance, collaboration, and resilience.

Coordination flourishes in alignment

The more aligned we are – on anything – the better we are in coordinating communication and work. In well-coordinated work and communication benefits exceed costs. The risks of tensions and delays are lower. Trust flourishes.

Teams work by tension or agreement

Agreements are mutually made and tested commitments to specific actions. They are based on shared experiments. Where teams lack agreements, there is the risk of spoken and unspoken tensions. Agreements make for more smooth sailing for everyone.

Big yeses result from successive small yeses

Yes is agreement. We build alignment one agreement at a time. We start with the smallest yeses and work our way into progressively larger yeses. Doing this builds confidence in our shared potential for alignment. When we say a team acts with courage we mean it acts with intentionally built confidence.

Visibility is responsibility

We construct a workplace where everything is visible. Anyone can at any time see what anyone else is working on, thinking, needing help with, and completing. This keeps the team in sync. People feel responsible for each other because they are visible to each other.

Velocity

The key to velocity is giving attention to it

What we give attention to grows. The more we talk about the timing of anything the more possible velocity becomes. Velocity breaks down and slows down when we don't talk enough about timing and instead just talk about assumptions and complaints. Timing is everything.

When it comes to communication, a pull environment has greater velocity and fewer costs than a push environment

In a pull environment, people who need to know something share their questions so people with information know exactly who needs something and when. This is more efficient than having people with information guess about who they need to push information to and when.

What we don't know is more important than what we do

We create solutions that work because we learn our way into them. Learning is leveraging our unknowns as questions that expand our knowing. Expanding our knowing leads to useful solutions. It begins with leveraging what we don't know as a prime asset.

Waiting is the enemy of the good

Any kind of waiting for anything is a drag on velocity and a generator of unaffordable and unnecessary costs. This means waiting for assignments, approvals, permissions, help, feedback, ideas, updates. Waiting is not an opportunity for blame and excuses but a chance to redesign how things work.

Learning

We learn our way into a future we want to see

No matter how many goals we set and plans we make we create a new future by learning our way into it. What matters is a growth mindset. The work of a team is to create the best possible shared future together. We make this possible through relentless and resilient learning.

Learning is the engagement of strengths

Each individual and shared achievement comes about because we have engaged the right chemistry of existing strengths at the right time. Talking about what we call weaknesses, flaws, and deficiencies is an opportunity to also talk about what strengths we can engage in any kind of new learning.

People do what they can based on what they know at the time

As human beings, we are not as complex as we might seem. We do what we know. We always do what we can based on what we know at the time. Doing differently requires knowing differently. This is why learning is everything.

Feedback works when people feel valued

No matter how important or useful the feedback we have for others it will be well received if people feel valued by us. When people feel valued, they feel open to insights from others. The varieties of ways to help others feel valued and valuable are countless.

When it comes to learning, no two brains are wired the same

Neuroscience makes it clear that no two brains are wired in the same way from their experience. Each brain processes information differently. This is why telling people what makes sense to us doesn't make sense to them until they go through the process of putting it into their own words and into their thinking habits.

Warnings and threats close minds

As much as they might seem necessary, warnings and threats close minds to new inputs, learning, perspectives, possibilities, and opportunities. They have no power to create genuine and sustainable commitments or agreements. Only empathetic support does.

Assumptions make new opportunities invisible

We are continuously surrounded by new opportunities for learning and progress. They are only visible when we are more curious than assumptive. Assumptions obscure our view of new possibilities. New questions reveal them.

We can be wrong and not know it

The insidious truth of being wrong is that, while we are wrong, we can't know we are. While being wrong, we feel right. Just knowing we could be wrong makes it possible to become right. We discover what was just beyond the horizon of our confidence.

Progress in learning is more important than perfection

Where perfection is only occasionally available, and at great costs, progress in learning is persistently available. Once know our learning questions we can make progress in steps and phases. A progress mindset honors the reality that anything new happens in iterations not instantaneously.

Change

Change is a constant; uncertainty is an asset

While we can do all the plotting and planning possible change continues to be a constant. Agile teams flourish in uncertainty because they translate all of their plotting and planning assumptions into actionable questions that pave the way in progress.

People do not resist change; they resist being changed

No one enjoys the victimhood of being changed. We genuinely and persistently prefer the agency of making change possible. We like solving problems. We like preventing them even more. We don't resist being engaged with this sense of responsibility in agency.

We can only change what we understand

Solving for any problem begins with empathy, understanding the context for the change we wish to create. Empathy is seeing the world through the eyes of others. We create what works because understand with empathy.

Change is best when we experiment our way into it

The most effective and ultimately efficient way to create change is through series of small experiments. Iterations of experiments teach us the best ways to make change especially when the path is intrinsically uncertain and unpredictable.

Change spreads and scales through social networks

Change spreads first from early adopters. As they are supported, they naturally engage the middle adopter people they know. Middle adopters naturally engage later adopter people they know. Change momentum begins with a prime focus on engaging and supporting early adopters.

Adoption and adaption happens in phases

We align with change at the rate we are capable of. We optimize this rate when we organize change in transparent and actionable phases. When we aren't overwhelmed, our alignment velocity is optimal.

Adoption moves at the speed of storytelling

Stories of progress and success inspire change alignment. They bring about optimism and the possibility of agency. They challenge fear, pessimism, and cynicism. They also inform the varieties of ways we can adapt change to our realities.

Generativity

Strong teams flourish in diverse perspectives

When perspectives are diverse and listening is strong, we flourish more as a team than when we strive for a more monotone environment. We are smarter when we each bring some measure of unique passions, experience, and talent.

People support what they help create

We support directions we help create. We support the design of work and workplaces we help create. We support decisions and solutions we help create. Support aligns us and brings out our best.

When it comes to creativity, quantity leads to quality

More ideas and questions lead to better ideas and questions. Debating over the best ideas postpones them because debating prevents the quantities of ideas. The focus on quantity removes filtering and unleashes a free flow of new possibilities and patterns.

Necessity is the mother of invention; dissent is its father

When we invite people to take a different approach to anything, we create more interesting things that work. New ideas flourish when we feel free to question even the most normative assumptions. Learning and engagement also become more possible.

Teams learn quickly that trusted leaders operate from specific and transparent principles in specific situations. This transparency builds trust with their leader and builds trust within the team as people also work from these principles.

The call for trusted leaders

It's interesting that, while some things are working well, others aren't. We see this at the scale of teams and organizations, industries and professions, cities and regions, states and nations.

We are becoming more aware that the leaders in each context have ordinary and extraordinary opportunities to shape success or struggle.

Trusted leaders do not necessarily have more or better resources than other leaders. They don't have more time or certainties. As other leaders invest time in trying to negotiate for more time and resources, trusted leaders are busy turning constraints into creative assets.

While we might be clear on the potentials of other leaders there are no clear boundaries on the potentials of trusted leaders and their trusted teams.

They are distinguished by how they think, act, and interact all of which are profoundly shaped by the language they use in their thinking, acting, and interacting.

The invitation here is to learn and practice the language of trusted leaders.

Language

The language of leadership

We usually open a new round of leader coaching with the same admonition: We are not going to change who you are. You are a gift to be engaged, not a problem to be fixed.

We will not give you tests so you have new boxes to put yourself in. You won't need boxes where you're going.

We don't have the time for or interest in fixing you. As radical as it might sound we're going to work with you just as you are.

Not only are you fine as you are, accepting yourself fully as you are will be a core requirement for any kind of new learning. Self-acceptance is a core competency in the quintessential empathy of being a trusted leader.

I learned this admonition from my mentors as they trained me in my twenties as an emerging psychotherapist and leader. Now the brain science behind this is most compelling.

We tell leaders in coaching that all they are going to do is learn a new language, a language that makes it easier for people to work together with vision, cohesion, courage, creativity, agility, velocity, trust, and relentless learning.

And that's what happens. They discover new levels of leadership through new levels of language. Everyone notices; they feel better, and the team performs at their best. Language has this power.

The neurosciences make it clear that doing follows knowing. We always do what we can based on what we know at the time. Our knowing is shaped by our language. When language shifts, knowing shifts, performance shifts.

Engaging language

It's curious why some teams are quite engaged while others are not. These engagement contrasts can exist even though these teams and their leaders are part of the same organization and have similar levels of competency, compensation, constraints, and conditions.

The difference is in how they feel about their work. As the latest brain science indicates, how they feel is shaped by their language.

When we study how these leaders sound, we hear distinct differences in what they say and ask.

Engagement is a function of language. A leader's language has the power to create the conditions for engagement and disengagement.

As trusted leaders, we use and invite engaging language. Engaging language has five distinguishing qualities. It is clear, humble, empathetic, encouraging, and respectful.

Clear

When we are clear in what we say and ask no one has to guess, interpret, or assume what we mean. No one has to worry about what's behind what we say. We are transparent; there is no hidden behind.

Clarity creates shared understanding. Shared understanding is authentic alignment. Alignment moves at the speed of clarity.

People trust people who are clear. Clear means specific, detailed, and factual. It gives us the kind of credibility and dependability that builds trust. People are engaged with us to the degree they trust us.

Clarity is also velocity. The more clear we are the more fluently talk moves into action.

Humble

As trusted leaders, we talk as much about what we don't know as what we do. We are known for asking questions that have not yet emerged. We are inspired and organized by our unknowns.

We do not fabricate convenient answers for the occasion because we think we have to have all the answers or be the smartest person in the room.

We take responsibility for what we fall short or fail on. We do not assign blame for our mistakes and errors nor do we take credit for the contributions of others.

Valuing the gifts of others, we ask for help, ideas, feedback, and support. This makes it easier for others on our team to do the same. Humility is about making it easier for others to feel valued by us. Rather than making us vulnerable, it makes us valuable.

Empathetic

We express genuine interest in how people feel. People trust others who care how they feel.

Empathy is validating the truth of someone's experience. We validate that their emotions make sense given what they know at the time. It is the opposite of dismissing or disregarding what they feel. Empathy is also helping people find their sense of agency. One way to do this is with a simple, engaging question: So, what's possible for you to do right now? It is among the most caring questions we can offer.

Knowing how people feel about anything is the practical basis for making things easier for them.

Encouraging

We encourage people to take initiative, try and learn new things, and work together instead of apart.

Especially when they might be hesitant to do so, we encourage them to give voice to their hopes, concerns, and questions. We encourage them to champion rather than cringe at change.

In the language of encouragement, we express explicit and sincere faith in their individual and shared ability to do well, get through something tough, and learn from experience.

When we show up with encouragement, people feel and act with a sense of trust in themselves. Teams flourish when people have faith in themselves and each other. With this kind of trust, they feel confident taking on what comes their way.

Respectful

As trusted leaders, we use language that expresses respect.

The language of respect is about agency. Agency is having a choice to say yes or no to a request or offer. In respect we invite, request, and offer rather than command, demand, or impose. Disrespect is denying someone a sense of agency.

Every human being on the planet knows clearly and immediately when they are given respect or disrespect.

We allow people choice because only with the ability to say a genuine no do they have the ability to say a genuine yes. A yes without the option of no is the deceit of compliance, not a genuine yes. Genuine engagement is a genuine yes.

People trust us as leaders when we show up with the language of respect. We show up with respect because it is easier for people to be their best selves when they feel respected.

Cliches, platitudes, and jargon

Team velocity and vibe are directly impacted by language successes and language breakdowns.

Language breakdowns have the character of cliches, platitudes, and jargon. The following are among the more brilliant examples of language breakdowns.

We need to line up all the arrows, get on the same page, get our ducks in a row. We need to hold people accountable, run it up the flagpole, go after the low hanging fruit. Let's not reinvent the wheel, and we don't need people rocking the boat.

We need to break down silos, push the envelope, and play hardball. You need to keep me in the loop, think outside the box, and take this off-line. My door is always open. Failure is not an option. It is what it is. We need to bucketize, cross-pollinate, socialize this, take a deep dive, reach out, not get too into the weeds, herd the cats, and circle the wagons.

We talk about *the paradigm shift, transformation, being data-driven, the win-win, team players, the parking lot, bandwidth, optics, step up to the plate, monetize, strategize, incentive, analyze, at the end of the day.*

We wax on about *the stake in the ground, line of vision, one-off, due diligence, move the needle, 30-thousand foot view, too many chiefs, scalable, best practices, competitive, push back, level-set, blocking and tackling, thrown under the bus, close the loop, re-org, market share, and run with this.*

In each instance, the language obscures more than it reveals. Even as it projects an aura of importance, it is more opaque than transparent. The language gives the appearance of saying something but nothing is being clearly understood.

Each begs for multiple interpretations that have the power to cause all manner of tensions, mistakes, and delays. Each is a variety of communication breakdown.

Our best response to the low-value language of cliches, platitudes, and jargon is curiosity. We ask for specifics behind the non-transparency of ambiguities, hoping specifics are waiting to be revealed. This minimizes and prevents communication breakdowns.

Trust optimizing and minimizing language

As leaders, everything we say and ask tends to optimize or minimize mutual trust.

Anything we say, ask, or do that implies others are here to serve us minimizes mutual trust and communicates disrespect. These create the conditions for people to feel powerless, defensive, and untrusting. The more they feel these the more likely it is they will take the same attitudes with others and struggle in their work.

As trusted leaders, we use and invite language that optimizes mutual respect and support. We explicitly and implicitly make it clear that this is a partnership environment.

We aren't anxious about the need for power over others. We don't need to be smarter than others. Our language is our power and empathy is our intelligence.

We are absolutely fine with everyone being their best selves together because they flourish in a mature environment of mutual respect.

Respect is shared decision making, information, and responsibility. When we succeed, we succeed together; when we fail, we fail together. We will often have more questions than answers and moving forward will always about the questions we share.

We use language that makes it easier for people to take initiative, think creatively and critically, collaborate rather than compete, and continuously learn.

This is what a mature trust-rich environment looks, sounds, and feels like. When we as leaders show up with maturity in obvious respect for others it makes it easier for them to show up with respect as well. They trust us because we are willing to be partners with them.

Tone and value

Language has two dimensions: tone and value.

Tone is the continuum between positive and negative. Positive tone opens up people's thinking; negative shuts it down. Negative tone drains energy making it harder for people to take initiative and collaborate well.

Positive tone creates energy, making it easier for people to be their best selves whatever reality is.

Everything we say and ask has tone. Everything has energy and emotional consequences. Positive and negative form a continuum.

Positive language is the language of optimism, encouragement, confidence, empathy, engagement, aspiration, interest, appreciation, welcoming, and support. It is the language of requesting, offering, and committing.

Negative language is the language of cynicism, complaint, criticism, rigidity, assumption, dismissal, suspicion, bullying, and threatening. It is the language of demanding, demeaning, blame, and excuse-making.

The essence of tone is our choice of words. Our choice of words influences what we feel and what we feel shapes what we say, ask, and do. Our choice of words also influences and shapes what others feel and do. That's the power of words.

When language shifts, emotions and actions shift. Leaders can maintain the status quo with a negative tone, especially when anxiously pressuring for change. New things are more possible with positive tone.

Value is the continuum between clear and unclear. High-value language is clear. It is specific and detailed. We don't have multiple interpretations of what someone says or asks. We have a single sense of it and it is the same sense they have as well.

Low-value language is unclear. It is ambiguous and vague. We can interpret it in multiple ways.

In positive tone and high-value language, we give people specific useful suggestions in their work that to them feel realistic and doable. In positive tone and low value, we give people vague congratulations like great job or something equally vague.

In negative tone and high value, we demean someone with critical details of their failure. In a negative tone and low value, we issue unspecified threats implying their job could be ambiguously on the line if things don't improve in unspecified ways.

When we as leaders see people react or respond to what we say or ask, we first look at our language as a potential contributor to what they feel and do.

Language tone

All language, even single words or phrases, have distinct vibes. Tone influences how people feel. How people feel influences how they perform, interact, and learn. Ultimately, how people feel determines their engagement and commitment.

When we see people doing well as a result of our language it can be because we got the tone right.

People tend to be more open and receptive to what we have to say and ask when our tone is more positive. They tend to be more closed and cautious when our tone is more negative.

Intentions don't directly impact people as much as language. Our intentions are intrinsically inaccessible to others. People only know the intentions we put into language for them.

If we want someone to trust our intentions they will get this through the explicit reality of our language.

Language value

When someone speaks in high-value language, we feel clear on what they're saying and implying. We don't have to endure the delays and costs of guessing, interpreting, hypothesizing, speculating, or assuming.

We don't have to poll others, walk on eggshells, or worry about taking apparent risks. We do these with low-value language.

A value fallacy is believing that when something is clear to us it is likewise clear to others. We assume when they say yes to our asking if they understand something their yes means they understand. There are many reasons why someone would say they understand what they do not.

We only know if someone understands something if they get right what we said in their language. Even people who think they know us well can get wrong what is unclear to them.

Low-value language can be word-heavy or word light, just as high value can be. The difference is how much interpretation people have to do relative to what we say and ask.

Low-value language includes things like: as soon as possible, done, responsible for, report to, out of scope, off track, beyond expectations, and overwhelmed. Even a simple yes or no can be low value. Details addressing who, what, when, how, why, where, how much or many give language high value.

Value is directly related to credibility. High value is more credible than low-value language.

To shift tone, shift language

It's possible to be tone aware and tone unaware. When tone aware, we're conscious of the emotional tone of our language.

The words yes, and, and could you have a distinctly different tone than no, but, and you will.

We notice when our choice of words sounds more alive or dull, engaged or tired, enthusiastic or bored, irritated or patient, annoyed or persistent, heavy or light, frustrated or determined, overwhelmed or focused.

When tone unaware, we aren't conscious of the tonal quality of our language. We assume our tone is fine as long as we're saying and asking what we want to say and ask.

You need to... is tonally different than *I have an ask that...* or *Would you be willing to...?*

I don't agree... is tonally different from *Can you tell me more about...* or *I could agree with this if...* or even *Would you consider a counter-offer that...?*

Do you have any idea that...? is tonally different than *What's your understanding about...?*

Not only do others feel differently hearing different language, we feel differently using it. Language is the core of emotion. When we change language, we change emotion.

When we want to feel and come across as less irritated or aggravated, all we need to do is experiment with different kinds of language. It starts with learning to be more tone aware.

Listening for the unspoken

When we talk with people in any situation and setting, we listen for the unspoken to make our language and theirs as high value as possible.

It's as important and interesting to listen to what isn't said as much as what is. There are reasons why something would go unsaid. These are nine of many possible.

We are concerned about how something might be received. We feel certain something will be refused, criticized, attacked, or dismissed. We have an opinion but no evidence to defend it if confronted.

We're concerned our tone might come across in a way that creates tension or misunderstanding. We think or know something in conflict with what others think.

We worry that if we are completely transparent it will not work in our favor. We don't think others are entitled to our perspective or opinion.

We have something negative or biased and don't want to come across as negative or biased. We aren't sure what we have to say makes complete sense and don't want to sound ignorant or incompetent.

Listening to the unspoken means listening for cues. These are qualifiers like maybe, to some degree, sometimes, some people, with mixed results. They are dissonances between what people say or ask and how they say or ask it, as when someone makes a declaration or commitment in a less than convincing tone.

We listen for language that is missing subjects, verbs, objects, modifiers, time frames, emotions, motivations, or implications. We can listen for unspoken hunches, guesses, curiosities, assumptions, or expectations others have.

Listen for means asking. We use simple questions to shift things from unspoken to spoken. Each expresses genuine interest that builds trust. People feel more welcome and comfortable speaking the unspoken when they trust us.

Can you say more about that?
What is it about...?
I'm curious about...?
What's an example of that?
When you say...are you thinking…?
I'm interested in understanding more about…

These are examples of clean questions in contrast to abusive, loaded, and rhetorical.

The conspicuous silence of leaders

Silence is also language. As with all forms of language, our silence as leaders is observed and interpreted. Silence is not speaking about or responding to something that has been said, asked, or done.

Others' perception of our silence is easily an unknown for us. We have no idea our not saying or asking something is being perceived by others as silence they're having to awkwardly interpret and navigate.

Depending on how well people know or don't know us, silence can be interpreted as agreement, disagreement, apathy, frustration, condescension, inaccessibility, non-transparency, or confusion. Silence has the power to shut conversations down, prevent psychological safety, provoke anxiety, and erode trust.

People who know us well might accurately interpret our silence but it is not guaranteed. People who don't know us well have the greatest risk of misinterpretation.

When it comes to silence management we have several options.

We track whether we are responding to what others say and ask what seems important to them. This includes anything they share in any media. This is one reason check-ins are useful: to keep up with what is most figural and relevant beyond the edges of our awareness.

We can speak up on what seems to be more important or sensitive to people on the team. We can respond to anything emotionally charged in conversations and meetings.

These effectively reduce the risks of misinterpretations and make open, respectfully constructive conversations more possible.

Language that weakens, erodes, and prevents trust

This is language that expresses and provokes negative emotions, defensiveness, denial, blame, shutting down, giving up, non-transparency, resistance to learning and change, division between people, an environment of mistrust and tension, and unproductive mindsets.

It includes:

- Lecturing, threatening, demeaning, criticizing, finger-pointing, or blaming
- Deflecting and not responding to questions, ideas, asks, offers, or complaints
- Defending and justifying what is unacceptable or worse for others
- Bullying people with accountability for things outside their direct awareness or control
- Attacking people with questions that leave them feeling uncomfortable, put on the spot, or cornered
- Communicating unclear, non-actionable, or contradictory expectations, assignments, or standards
- Condescendingly reminding people about what they already know
- Using sarcasm to thinly disguise irritability, criticism, or worse

It's any language people experience as being demeaning, bullying, unclear, irrelevant, or redundant. Anything opposite and other than these work to build, sustain, and deepen trust.

Hopefully, you're getting more clear on how the essence of being a trusted leader is all about your language. If you think being smart, charming, and hard-working are important, they can be, especially if you're striving for the status of a high-achiever.

When you make things easier for people to know, feel, and do you are trusted as a result. It opens space for trustworthiness.

Becoming more language-conscious

As much as we could guess what people get from our language, we can only guess. We cannot automatically know what anyone hears or understands. We only know when we ask. It's all about questions, neither assuming nor interpreting.

What about what you just heard makes sense, and what raises questions for you?
Do you have any different ideas or insights?
Can you tell me what your understanding of this is right now?

How are you feeling right now about what you're hearing?
Is there anything you would like to know more or be more clear about?

Each person processes what they hear through the ways their brain has been wired from experience and learning. No two brains are wired alike. No two people hear the same thing in the same ways.

Ten people can hear ten different interpretations of what one person says or asks. Until we hear what they hear, we have no idea what they hear.

We do not rely on predicting or surmising what someone else hears from what we say. Knowing this is the basis for being more language conscious.

8 language actions

Among our most important work as leader is to make it easier for people and teams to coordinate their work and learning.

To do this we use and invite 8 language actions: declarations, commitments, timing, agreements, requests, assessments, offers, and acceptances.

We call these language actions because of their ability to make things happen. When it comes to team performance, interaction, and learning, action makes things happen. Some language has the power of action.

We make things easier for people through language actions. Each facilitates understanding, initiative, energy, attention, momentum, support, alignment, and sync.

Declarations

A declaration is a true statement. It is accurate in that the one who offers it can produce evidence of its truthfulness. It is explicitly and intrinsically not assumptive, speculative, or opinionated.

Its source can be direct or reported experience or observation. Declarations build trust. They make us reliable sources of knowing that support the success and well-being of others.

The language of declaration can sound like: *What I know for sure is that...* and *What I don't yet know for sure is...*

Notice we speak our personal truth with I rather than we. We can use we if those included in the we are named. We also don't disguise or exaggerate our truth with vague and misleading references to everybody, some people, they, always, and never.

Declarations are useful to support proposals, question assumptions, and shift perspectives. They can also help shift tone away from accusatory and defensive.

Commitments

A commitment is a promise. It is a promise to start, work on, review, resolve, decide, look into, confirm, request, communicate, schedule, follow up, follow through, or complete something. Trust equity is built and banked by making explicit, credible, and kept promises.

The opposite is making people assume, expect, or hope for something from us that we are not explicitly making a commitment about. An assumed commitment is not a commitment. It is a language breakdown. They should know what to expect by now is one version of this breakdown.

We make it as specific as we can, staying as credible and realistic as possible. When we lack complete specifics we say so. We communicate what is yet unclear or unknown to us even as we make a commitment. This gives integrity to our commitments.

We are specific in doneness and timing expectations. If a commitment we make is also somehow contingent on what others do we make this clear and make any relevant requests.

We have the confidence to move forward on a commitment when there is explicit acceptance from others to whom we're making promises. We don't assume acceptance in the absence of its explicit expression.

High integrity commitments are realistic. They are based on the realities of our willingness, ability, and capacity. They are not qualified with the language of hope-to, maybe, or possibly.

They are not just statements of willingness, as in *I can...* which doesn't exactly have the clarity of *I will* or *You will have...by...* They are made and accepted with honesty and confidence.

Timing

Timing is clarifying when things are estimated or known to start, restart, and complete. Things include tasks, reviews, acceptances, check-ins, huddles, work sessions, and help.

Communicating timing is important for any work that involves multiple eyes and hands. Getting and staying in sync means knowing how everyone engaged in a deliverable is thinking about timing. For teams, time management is timing management.

Things start and complete too early and too late when timing is unshared and off. Timing is an agreement. No one can decide for everyone because no one knows all the variables that factor into the timing of things.

Agreements

Agreements are mutual commitments to action based on shared experiments. Agreements help things go smoothly.

We talk about what matters to us in this situation or this kind of situation. We name what we have in common on this. We name all the potential benefits of these coming true.

Then we propose whatever we think we could experiment with to make possible these things that matter to us here. For each proposal, we talk about any possible exceptions and how these would be accommodated.

We together decide on the details and duration of the experiment. After the experiment, we do a critique together: *What happened well and why? What did we learn? What commitment are we now ready to go ahead with?*

Agreements are optimal in any situations of misalignment, tension, and breakdowns. They are the opposite of dictates and mandates imposed on people. These are mutually crafted and tested commitments. They prevent and minimize tension which is useful because tension is a drag on velocity.

Requests

Requests are asks. We request information, ideas, questions, proposals, counter-proposals, acceptances, help, support, introductions, and commitments.

Information can be situational, technical, procedural, and organizational. We can ask for ideas on a problem or issue. We can ask for questions when moving our thinking forward.
We can ask for proposals, counter-proposals, and acceptances to move action forward.

We can ask for help with an assignment, issue, question, or problem. We can ask people to support any effort we are engaged in.

We ask for introductions when we want to learn from or with others who have talents, experience, or knowledge that some effort requires.

We ask people to commit to assignments when we think they are capable of and available for them. This is the language of Can you...? and Would you be willing to..?

Requests make it easier for others to also do so. We want to send the message that it's perfectly OK to be dependent on and interdependent with others.

Requests are necessary, not optional. We make them without pressuring others into compliance. We make asks without knowing how they might or will be received. Just making an ask is an indicator of respect and as such strengthens trust.

We notice who is and isn't making requests. People can fail to make requests for several reasons. They don't want to bother or burden others. They don't want to appear less than self-sufficient and independent. They lack trust that others will deliver according to their standards.

We must encourage people to make requests. They cannot get certain things done without the support of others. The costs of uncommunicated requests are delays and tensions.

Assessments

Assessments are comparisons of outcomes and standards. They can be prescriptive and descriptive. A standard is a level of doneness in any assignment.

Three simple standards are: great, good, and not yet. When we make any kind of assessments, we are explicitly comparing actual outcomes with expected standards. Standards can be established by mandate, agreement, or norm.

Mandates are non-negotiables like public regulations, corporate bylaws, or organizational policies. Agreed on standards are mutually negotiated and shared sets of rules, algorithms, principles, or practices. Norms are what through experience or folklore has been established as the right way things happen and get done.

Standards can be communicated with and without exceptions. Good performance relies on a clear understanding of standards. Explaining the activities of an assignment can occur with or without the clarification of standards. It helps to talk equally about what unacceptable looks like.

The language of assessments can sound like: *If we consider x as good, I think this outcome hits the mark because...* and *If we consider x as good, I think this outcome misses the mark because....*

When an assessment includes detailed examples it is grounded. It's even better if both the giver and receiver of the assessment consider the examples relevant, accurate, and useful.

Grounded assessments feature high-value language. When examples are absent, irrelevant, inaccurate, or not useful, an assessment is ungrounded. People take grounded assessments seriously. They don't take ungrounded assessments seriously.

When we are the recipient of an ungrounded assessment, we have several possible moves. We can thank people for their assessment. We can express any agreement we have. We can ask for more examples for any cited actions or outcomes.

We can ask for more examples of standards. We can ask for clarity on exceptions. We can ask if they have any requests, offers, or proposals.

Offers

An offer is a proposal. We offer to share declarations, assessments, questions, updates, ideas, collaboration, assignments, and help. Unlike imposing, offering is respectful. It precedes giving and moves forward with explicit acceptance.

We share what we offer after it is accepted by others. The language of offers includes: Would you like if I ..?, Would you be interested in...?, and Can I offer you…?

Offering makes genuine receptivity possible. No one can be genuinely receptive to what they don't have a choice about receiving. They can only react with the tension of compliance or refusal.

Offers can have the character of invitations. We invite people to consider acceptance of something we offer.

When offers are refused, and we are clear the refusal will incur unaffordable costs, we can make a counter-offer if possible. We can redirect our offer to someone else if someone else is available. In the meantime, our work is to make it easier for people to give words to the basis of their refusal.

Others might believe that acceptance of an offer might create problems for them they aren't prepared to bypass or solve. We can ask about the costs to them or others in accepting our offer: Do you see this creating any issues for you or others?

We can ask if they have counter-offers. We can adjust our offer based on what we discover in these conversations. It is all distinctively respectful.

Acceptances

Acceptance is agreement with something committed, offered, or shared. It is something we approve as good or great, as done rather than not yet done. OK, great, and thanks are acceptances

In high-value language acceptances we are specific about why we are accepting. In low-value language acceptances, we share vague reasons for our acceptance or no reasons at all.

Instead of acceptance, we can respond to these with counter-offers and refusals. These can also be with high or low-value language.

High-value language is particularly useful in refusals and unresolved negotiations of offers and counter-offers. Counter-offers can feature different versions of scope, cost, and timing.

When we tell people we are accepting something they offering or deliver, it's a prime opportunity to highlight what matters to us and why. This builds everyday trust through shared values.

The timing of language actions

Declarations are useful in conversations abundant in assumptions. They can challenge unquestioned beliefs. They can inspire and encourage optimism and confidence. They support ideas, requests, and proposals. They answer questions for more clarity.

Commitments are useful when we want others to know exactly what they can expect from us. They can correct unrealistic expectations. They make our action-taking more possible. When kept, they build trust.

Timing is useful when we want to coordinate actions between or among people. It proactively prevents the disconnects of balls dropping and toes stepped on. Things have a better chance of getting done on time when timing is good from beginning to end.

Requests are useful when we want to engage someone in an assignment, task, or conversation. We might not know someone's availability until we make an ask. Requests prevent assuming. They are respectful invitations that make commitments easier and more genuine for others.

Assessments are useful when we want people to be crystal clear on the distinctions of great, good, and not yet relative to anything they communicate, do, and deliver. They are helpful when people are struggling and when they are doing well.

Offers are useful when we want someone to consider our ideas, assessments, support, or help. Like requests, we don't know about another's receptivity to something until we offer it. Offers respectfully prevent assumptions about receptivity.

Acceptances are useful when we want people to know we appreciate what they say, ask, and do. They create and confirm a shared sense of doneness and value. They prevent others from assuming our acceptance or refusal. They help people feel valued and respected.

Language breakdowns

Each of the 8 language actions has corresponding language breakdowns. These include assumptions, excuses, disconnects, expectations, demands, criticisms, coercions, and denials.

Assumptions

In contrast to the factual nature of declarations, assumptions don't require evidence of fact.

People can present assumptions as expectations, speculations, hypotheses, or predictions. They are best, plausible, or wild guesses about what we lack data about.

When people don't qualify them as assumptions we can misinterpret them as declarations of fact. This can cause any manner of communication and action breakdowns.

When people say things that are ambiguously not clear declarations, we can ask:

What do we know for sure?
How do we know that?
Could something else be true?
What unknowns exist around this?
Could there be anything else to the story?
Does anyone know more about this than we do?

Instead of the ambiguous *I think...* we can frame assumptions with It's possible that... and *I don't know if...* Assumptions are ideal ways to identify our next questions.

Excuses

Excuses are expressions of pessimism in response to an ask. Instead of making a commitment to something we cite reasons why we don't think we can. The language of excuses includes: I don't see how I could… and That would be difficult because…

Whether they are delivered in a sincere, convincing, and apologetic tone, they are justifications for inaction people hope we accept.

We can reactively deliver excuses and hope others back off from further requesting or expecting commitments. We can proactively create excuses with frequent complaints about how overwhelmed we are.

We can respond to excuses with requests for offerings, commitments, and agreements.

Is there anything else you could offer here?
Is there anything you feel confident committing to here?
What would need to be true for you to offer or commit to this?
Are there any agreements we could make here?

Disconnects

This is when everyone collaborating on any deliverable decides on their own when they will start, work on, and complete things.

This effectively limits the potentials for everyone being in sync. Sync requires shared communication and agreements on timing so momentum is optimal.

Things do not necessarily complete on time because people have deadlines and they're all working hard. Things complete on time because they get momentum right. They get momentum right because they get timing right together.

To shift people from disconnects to timing we can ask:

When are all the tasks involved here estimated to begin and complete?
Are there any factors that could make any of these estimates change?
How are updates being communicated and adjustments made?

Expectations

Expectations are presumptions about what others will do. We have expectations in the absence of commitments, agreements, and offers. People can have spoken and unspoken expectations of each other. As assumptions expectations make tensions more possible.

In the worst cases, someone discovers another's unspoken expectation by not satisfying it. People who believe in common sense tend to be those with the most unspoken expectations. For them, the list is long of things that go without saying.

When people operate from expectations, we can ask:

What are your expectations here?
What are you assuming could, should , or will happen?
What leads you to assume these?
What do you want or need to happen here?
Do you have a specific request or proposal for an agreement?

Absent explicit and mutually shared requests and agreements, expectations create optimal conditions for costly tensions, disconnects, and disappointments that weaken and erode trust.

Demands

In contrast to requests, demands leave people with the option to comply or refuse. Requests open the conversation; demands close it.

While requests give people the agency to respond honestly to our asks, demands imply loyalty or disloyalty, obedience or disobedience. Questioning is out of the question as a signal of disloyalty.

Demands issue non-negotiable expectations with implications of imposed consequences for compliance or refusal.

Several responses to demands are possible:

What's not certain for me here is...
My saying yes to this would mean that...
Is anything about this negotiable?
What are the standards of great, good, and not yet for this?

When it's clear that we get demands from people who aren't clear on their unknowns, it's our job to help them identify and work from these. Requests are only possible when we are realistic.

Criticisms

Criticisms tell others what's wrong without clarifying the basis for judgment. Unlike assessments, they are complaints that don't include clarifying the standards not met.

For example I didn't appreciate when you said... or It bothers me when you... or I just don't understand why you insist on...

We can respond to criticism with:

What were you expecting, hoping, or needing?
How were you inconvenienced by those not happening?
Is there anything else I should know?
Can you help me be clear on how you define great, good, and not yet here?

Would you accept my offer to...?

Coercions

In contrast to offerings, coercions deliver what others have not requested. This includes giving people unrequested feedback, ideas, opinions, questions, and suggestions. It is a cousin to demands. As demands try to dictate action, coercions try to dictate thinking,

Both disrespectfully keep people from the freedom to accept, refuse, or negotiate. They force people into the tension of untenable compliance or non-compliance.

Coercion is the imposition of opinion for conversion. People do not feel free to question, resist, or refuse what is imposed or would at some cost.

We can respond to coercion with:

What makes sense to me here is...
What raises questions for me here is...
What would be most useful to me here is...
Would you be willing to also consider...?

Denials

In denials people do not even acknowledge something offered, proposed, or delivered. It is neither explicitly accepted nor refused. It is essentially ignored.

When something we say, ask, or do goes unacknowledged we are wise to be more curious than assumptive. If someone has a pattern of denials with us they might do the same with others, also causing communication tensions and breakdowns.

Everyone benefits from our explicitly responding to denials as soon as they occur.
We can respond to denials with:

What you think about this… is important to me because…
Is this… useful to you?
If not, is there something else you would consider?

Accessible language

Language actions are accessible language. Accessible means easy to understand.

It is easier to respond well to declarations than opinions, commitments than excuses, timing than disconnects, agreements than expectations, requests than demands, assessments than criticisms, offers than coercions, and acceptances than denials.

When people experience our language as accessible, they experience us as accessible. Accessibility makes us trustworthy.

The accessibility of language actions makes it easier for people to feel respected, creating the conditions for them to respect us and others.

We create an environment of trust and respect each time we model and invite any of the language actions. Inviting dialogue is another way to do this.

Dialogue

Dialogue is an alternative to monologue and debate.

Monologue is when people dominate a conversation with a ramble, rant, or lecture. No one feels comfortable joining in or being left out. It is a disrespectful disregard for the perspectives, questions, talents, and time of others. As a leader, we can redirect by engaging others.

Debate is a competition for being right. It is often structured with an either-or question. It sets up the possibilities for costly win-lose or lose-lose outcomes.

The agenda in a debate is to make others wrong to seize the prize of being right. It comes from and breeds non-trust and mistrust.

We can intervene by reframing the conversation as a both-and question: *How could both be somehow possible?*

We offer and share our ideas. We give people time with the question since they are likely not prepared for it.

It is also helpful to soften the edges of everyone's thinking with *What are your hopes and concerns around this?* Then, we can invite people to think of ways to make some of these hopes more possible and some of these concerns less possible.

Dialogue is a conversation where everyone is interested in shared learning. Learning is a priority over attacking or defending, debating, or deflecting.

Learning happens on two levels. We learn from each other, taking in new insights and ideas. We learn together, crafting ideas that we could only craft together, that no one of us could craft alone.

We invite dialogue with questions like: *What could we learn from each other and together?* and *What kinds of questions does all of this raise?*

The shift from debate to dialogue gets everyone on the same side of the table in the direction of a both-and win-win.

Debate diminishes trust and makes everyone less smart together. Dialogue builds trust and makes everyone smarter together.

Direction

The big picture

The more people are clear on the big picture, the more able they are to contribute to it.

The big picture is the direction we're headed as an organization and as a team. It describes intended achievements, impacts, and growth.

Clarity in our shared big picture creates clarity of progress. A sense of progress is one of the cornerstones for meaning and joy in work.

When people don't see and share the big picture their velocity is slow, costs are high, complaints are many, mindsets are fixed, change is resisted, and engagement is low. The big picture is a big deal.

Context

Context is the dynamic space of variables beyond our team that impacts and influences our experience, contributions, and costs. Clarity on the big picture requires clarity on our context.

As a team we track trends within and beyond our organization. Beyond includes the dynamics of our markets, industries, regulations, economics, fundings, and investments.

We update this view of our context on a regular basis using whatever direct and indirect research methods available.

What's shifting and changing and why?
What's not shifting and changing and why?
What's happening that is impacting and could impact our team?
What should we be paying close attention to?

We use what we learn to create and refresh our direction as a team.

Team identity

Team identity is a shared sense of who we are as a team. Before we have this, everyone has their unaligned versions. Aligned identity is core to team cohesion, direction, contribution, and velocity.

Here are some questions that help shape the conversation.

What makes this team different than other teams in the organization?
What does it have in common with other teams?
If someone observed and listened in on us working and interacting for a month, what would they say seems important to us as a team?

What matters to us as we work and learn together?
How would you finish the statement: We are a team who...?
What do we want people to say about us behind our backs?

It's important to capture all common elements in response to these questions shared by the team. It's useful to revisit and update all of it on a regular basis and to share it all with any new team members and significant team partners.

Principles

Principles act as our decision compass. They are the shared core beliefs that shape all of our decisions as a team. They describe our sense of how things work. They are rooted in our shared sense of team identity.

Our core beliefs are compelling and imperative for doing our best individually and as a team. One essential difference between high and low-velocity teams are the principled beliefs they make decisions from.

Here are some questions to make it easier for your team to name its core beliefs:

What are our beliefs about why we do well as a team when we do well as a team?
What are our beliefs about how we grow and develop as a team?
What values are implied in each of these beliefs?

Once we have shared core principles, we can consider how they can be a compass in our decisions as a team.

What kinds of decisions do we want to make based on our shared principles?
Which shared principles will help us in each decision category?

When we talk through team decisions, we check back on our principles so they inform our thinking, doing, and learning.

Mission

Our team mission is our shared reason for being. It's why we exist.

One form of mission is as a question rather than statement. Questions can be more inspiring and engaging than statements. One root form for a mission question is: What would it look like to…? Mission questions are questions we answer in the everyday doing of what we do as a team.

Here are some mission shaping questions:

What are we committed to doing that no one else is doing?
What would we like to be doing better or different than what anyone else is doing?
What are our promises to our markets and stakeholders?
What problems do we work every day to solve for?

It's a good idea for the team to revisit the mission question on a regular basis, particularly as we grow in understanding our place and purpose in the world.

Vision

Vision is what we want the future to look like given our reason for being. It is aspirational. One root form for a vision question is: How could we make it possible for...?

Here are some vision shaping questions:

What kinds of impacts would we love to see and make possible?
What kind of growth are we committed to making possible?
What do we want to become known for beyond what we are already known for?

With mission and vision, we generate as many possibilities as we can and then narrow them down based on what we share as priorities in common. While mission questions can be singular, vision questions can be plural.

Direction

Direction is what we are committed to creating together in the future to realize our mission and vision.

Direction is not an assumption, prediction, or speculation. It is an agile set of commitments. Agile means these will be refreshed on a regular basis based on our learning and the constant of change we experience in our team, organization, and world.

Unlike goals which are locations to arrive at, directions are lenses revealing new opportunities and possibilities in the present. The farther out in time we go to set directions the larger our lens on the present.

It's good practice to go out at least 20 years, far beyond current worries and constraints. This keeps us proactive more than reactive. We keep our context, identity, mission, and vision in mind as we work on direction.

What would we love to see and make possible over the next two decades?
What impossible would we love to see and make possible?

The idea is to generate as many options as we can, look for patterns, name the dominant patterns, and turn them into a handful of direction questions. These questions are compelling, credible, and clear.

One direction question form is a classic design thinking frame: How can we..? Shared direction designs our future together.

Translations

We translate our directions into specific 2-year progress indicators and then we translate these indicators into 2-quarter projects.

What indicators would tell us in two years that we are making progress in our directions?
What projects could we begin in the next two quarters that would give us momentum in these areas of progress?

These questions facilitate the engagement invitations and commitments to realize our directions. People on the team sign up for the projects they are most interested in from contribution and learning perspectives. We work on projects in the order of what makes practical sense.

Indicators include stories and statistics. Projects include experiments, research, development, proposals, and launches.

We refresh everything every two quarters since most planning assumptions are reliable for about that long. The process keeps us continuously inspired, focused, proactive, aligned, agile, and realistic.

Scenario learning

For each direction we commit to there is any number of unknowns. Unknowns include unpredictable types of change and opportunity scenarios.

We can identify some of these scenarios in two ways: imagining and researching.

We can imagine what could happen based on our resident experience, knowledge, and intuition. We can research current, cyclical, and emerging trends. Keeping our context in mind, we generate as many possible scenarios as we can. We choose a few to work with from three questions:

Which have greater apparent likelihood?
Which might have a greater impact on our team?
Which do we want to be prepared for?

For each scenario, we identify all the questions they raise and do any research we can to get insights into answers. We make our questions list more complete by turning any of our hopes, wishes, speculations, assumptions, and concerns into questions.

We use our new scenario learning to revisit our directions and progress indicators for any relevant adjustments, edits, and additions. We revisit scenario learning on a regular basis.

Goals and objectives

Many organizations continue the tradition of trying to set direction and coordinate work through goals and objectives.

Because they are assumption-based, goals and objectives have the most validity and reliability in stable, static, and predictable contexts. They are less so in use contexts that are new, dynamic, or uncertain.

If you are expected to submit or present your team's goals and objectives, you can use your 2-year indicators as your goals and 2-quarter projects as your objectives.

It is useful to attach the team's relevant knowns and unknowns for each goal and objective to keep the language high value and expectations more on the realistic side. Frame unknowns as questions.

Lack of useful direction from "the top"

In many organizations, people operate from the assumption that direction must come from the top. It's typically the only way they know. There are several reasons why it might not happen.

The senior team might be too unaligned or competitive to form a shared direction. They might share a risk-aversion that makes the status quo the default direction.

The language they use to describe direction might be of so low value that no one knows what it means in terms of action. They could assume people should be able to interpret direction from their coordinated and uncoordinated actions and decisions.

However your senior team is focused or floundering, as a trusted leader it's important to keep your team clear on and committed to its scope of influence.

Whatever happens at the top, we work as a team from our own shared, realistic, agile big picture. This is what it means to show up and contribute as a high integrity, trusted team.

Velocity

Sync

Staying in sync as a team is a week to week, day to day, and hour to hour coordination of work. When work is well-coordinated, several things are true.

Everyone knows what everyone is working on and where it currently is in relation to doneness and timing. This makes possible the real-time and on-time sharing of updates, help, and dot-connecting.

Things happen at the right time. Things start on time, meaning giving enough time for the next thing to start and complete on time. Everyone is clear on the sequence of work and what needs to happen prior to something else happening.

Adjustments are made quickly. If something changes, it's communicated so adjustments can be made and communicated.

Notice that sync is completely about communication: the flow of commitments, questions, offers, requests, and updates.

If sync is a new conversation for your team you can begin with these questions:

What tends to go well on our team now and why?

What are all the ways the right communication at the right time makes these easier to happen?
What can get stuck, delayed, bottlenecked, or redone?
How could communication make these less likely?

With each question, use any of the 8 language actions to explore the possibilities.

Updates

Whatever the size and complexity of an organization or team, change is a constant.

The list of what does and can change is not insignificant. This includes what others are starting, working on, completing, getting stuck in, needing help with, adjusting, or learning. It includes what needs an answer, decision, clarification, resolution, assignment, commitment, offer, request, acceptance, or delivery.

It's also keeping our pulse on all the relevant dynamics, patterns, and events outside our team and outside the organization. Our work has relevance to the degree we stay relevant.

In conversations with team members and the team, we ask for updates to make sure we're all working from the same understanding of what's changing inside and outside the team. This makes sync more possible.

The most basic update question is: *What's going on with...?*

This could be about a project, process, action, question, or issue. We listen for what people share, offer any questions and perspectives we have and invite other people's questions and perspectives.

We are always interested in context about anything going well or struggling: *Why and how is it that…?*

We want a shared understanding of what's shifting, changing, or new as well as clarity on why and how: What do we know is contributing to this? These are our knowns.

We surface any of our unknowns: *What are our assumptions, speculations, hunches, theories, hypotheses, and explanations about why and how things are as they are?* Then we ask people to turn these into questions and get as many answered as possible.

We can also identify our unknown unknowns with: *Is there anyone else beyond our team who could or would have a different sense of why and how things are as they are?* Another version is: *Who do we think knows the most about this? For both: What are their unknowns?*

Then we invite people on the team to ask these identified people for their insights, perspectives, and questions.

Huddles

Huddles are brief, 5-10 minute spontaneous or scheduled synchronous check-ins. They are proactive ways to make it easier for people to connect dots, request and offer help, and share relevant updates. They keep people in sync on interdependencies and timing.

They can happen virtually, in person, by phone, and through group text. We can have whole team huddles and huddles with any combinations of people on the team.

The only rule of thumb is that no work gets done in huddles. If things come up that require more conversation or a work session, that's scheduled during the huddle for another time.

Anyone on the team can call a spontaneous, focus-specific huddle. The only rule is that only those relevant to the focus are engaged, meaning no passive observers.

Assignment requests

On self-organizing teams, the default agreement on assignments is simple: If something needs to be done, no one is yet working on it, and you can do it, then you do it and communicate you are doing it.

It is also common practice for people to have standing and rotating assignments.

When we as leaders become aware of anything that needs to be handled or done we work from a bias for making make assignment requests rather than giving people assignments. This can sound like: *Can you...?* in contrast to *I'm assigning you to...*

If someone questions or refuses a request we can ask: *Is there anything you think could make this possible for you to do?* and *Is there someone else you think could be available for this?*

If it can be postponed, we can propose a counter-offer question: *Could you do this if it could start and complete when you could?*

You can invite others on the team to also make assignment requests to you and others on the team. No one and no velocity benefits from you being an assignment request bottleneck on the team.

When outlining upcoming work in the next month, quarter, or phase of a project, you can engage the team in a few basic questions:

Which assignments would play to everyone's strong areas?
Which assignments would play to everyone's learning questions?
Which most and least favorite assignments could be rotated?

You can also engage the team in making agreements on who to go to first for typical assignment requests based on the answers to these questions.

Who to go to first people can be those who have the most experience with an assignment. When multiple people are fairly equally experienced, the first responders can rotate assignments.

People who want learning, practice, and experience on any type of assignment get paired with those who have more mastery.

If someone shows a pattern of struggling with an assignment, we make sure they get the learning they need to progress toward doing well with it.

We provide the learning or ask another team member to provide it. All learning is captured, shared, and archived on short videos and checklists for future uses.

New technologies

Whether your team is adopting new technology platforms and apps or choosing their own to use, here are some useful questions:

What is everyone's understanding of the potential benefits of this technology?
Is everyone clear when we all need to be proficient with it?
Where is the tech already being used well?
Does anyone consider themselves to be early adopters or local experts with any of the tech?
Could anyone teach anything to anyone else on the team?
Are there people beyond the team who could teach anything?
Is anyone experiencing any level of reluctance or resistance with any technologies?
Do we need any agreements on when and how tech will be used?

We answer these through conversations, decisions, and experiments. We especially make sure more expert people are paired with less expert for optimal learning velocity.

Organizing chaos

Chaos comes in myriad forms. It's anytime uncertainties outnumber certainties. We find ourselves having more unknowns than knowns.

This happens with any significant changes inside or outside the team's world. It happens when we take on any kind of planning. It happens at the beginning of new projects, project phases, quarters, and years.

Three questions help us organize the chaos.

What do we want to ultimately be true?

Ultimately can be defined in whatever timeframe makes sense. Whether our sense of true is more or less clear, to begin with, our sense of this will shift as we learn our way forward.

What are our knowns and unknowns?

Knowns are data or research-based facts, things we have evidence for or things trusted others have evidence for. If it's not entirely clear if something is a known, treat it as an unknown.

Unknowns include assumptions, speculations, predictions, hypotheses, guesses, hunches, and opinions.

What are our questions and actions?

We turn any actionable unknowns into questions we can answer through research, decisions, and experiments. We do whatever we can to answer our questions. Answers lead to the next actions and outcomes as well as to the next questions. We engage whoever can help with these actions.

We answer questions in the order that makes sense. We work on them with a specific sense of momentum like daily and weekly. We keep updating our lists of questions.

As we keep iterating these three questions, we learn our way into more clarity one question at a time. New knowns lead to new unknowns; new answers lead to new questions. We do well keeping the chaos organized.

When we turn the challenge of uncertainty into the assets of questions we can navigate any kinds of chaos and change we encounter.

Toe stepping and ball dropping

Until work is well-synced, we can step on each other's toes and balls get dropped.

In toe stepping, one person takes on something someone is already working on. In ball dropping, people assume others are handling something.

Both are proactive communication opportunities, using questions like these:

When are stepping on each other's toes and letting balls drop possible?
Is it ever unclear or conflicting about whose work is what?
What kinds of typical asks and issues come up in our work and do we have agreements on how we sync up on these?
What would an experiment look like?
What could we make an agreement on?

Aligned and agile

Apps and algorithms make optimal alignment and agility possible.

Apps are digital tools for requesting, offering, sharing, organizing, and archiving anything that comes up for and from people on the team.

These include document apps like Google Docs and One Note, group messaging apps like Slack and Teams, whiteboard apps like Mural, and workflow and project management boards like Trello, Planner, and Monday.

They are well worth the time it takes to learn them. Introduce functions a few at a time. This makes learning easier. As always, video any teaching. Loom is a good app for this.

Algorithms are if-then rules related to any aspects of the work. The idea is to create agreements on what's optimal in each if situation. It creates a proactive approach to typically reactive situations.

Ifs can be routine and non-routine events, changes, issues, problems, and questions. Keep this list accessible, editable, and regularly updated as good and better practices emerge.

What can tend to happen unpredictably in our work?
When can we be more reactive than proactive?
For each of these ifs, what would be optimal then approaches?

Just getting people talking about how they react and respond to situations reveals functional and dysfunctional variations in approaches. It makes more alignment possible.

Outlining work

Because the whole idea of planning work can be fraught with costly assumptions, a useful alternative is talking about outlining work.

Outlining answers the questions: *Who will do what?* and *When will they do it?* They are commitment rather than assumption conversations.

We outline work in each of four categories: processes, decisions, projects, and workflows.

A process is something that repeats on a regular basis. It has inputs, steps, and outputs. The steps are optimally represented in checklists.

What processes do we have in place now?
How well is each performing?
Should we update any?
Do we have checklists for all processes?
What new and revised checklists could we experiment with or implement?

A decision is an answer to questions that address new situations and exceptions including problems, issues, conflicts, choices, and opportunities.

What decisions are in progress now?
Does anything need a decision now that is not being worked on?
Do we have any upcoming decisions we need an individual, a subgroup of people, or the whole team to work on?

With any decisions identified:

Who knows the most relative to this decision?
What questions should we be working from?
What are our hopes and concerns about the outcomes of this decision?
What needs to be true when this decision is made and moved into action?

A project is a unique effort that produces non-repeated deliverables like research, products, services, programs, and approaches.

What active projects do we have now?
How are they performing?
Should we re-visit outlining the work in them for better performance?
Does the work for any new projects need to be outlined or launched?

A workflow is a calendar of work that can include tasks, decisions, and projects.

We can outline work in a workflow for each week, month, and quarter. On a higher level we can sketch workflows for multiple quarters and for the year.

Outlining a workflow answers 7 questions.

What will get done in this timeframe?
Who are we doing it for and why do they need it?
What will doneness in terms of great, good, and not yet look like for them and us?
Who will get it done and when will it start and complete?
What knowns and unknowns are we starting with?

Keep work outlining agile. Revisit and revise any work outlines based on things that are changing, working well, or struggling along with what we are learning from experience.

The visible workplace

The more everyone's outlined and real-time work is visible, the more a team is in sync.

In a visible workplace everyone can see and have conversations about how work is outlined and the status of everyone's work.

This is the opposite of a disconnected and non-transparent workplace where people try to manage sync through individual texts, emails, files and folders, meetings, and reports.

We create seamless visibility with digital tools like channel-based group text apps, workflow boards, and whiteboards.

A few questions help to get things rolling:

Is everyone keeping their visibility up to date?
Does anyone want to ask for or offer help with any of the technology tools we are using?
Do we need any new agreements on how we're using our tools to stay in sync?

Bottlenecks

A bottleneck is when anything in a process or project becomes stuck waiting for action, resources, approvals, resolutions, handoffs, or deliveries. They are not always obvious.

We start by identifying any bottleneck patterns:
Is anyone ever waiting for something to start or complete?
For each example is waiting a matter of delays in action, resources, approvals, or resolutions?
What could remove these bottlenecks?
What can and will we experiment with?

Sprints

Sprints are 10-20 minute live conversations that organize two-week workflows. They are simple structures featuring four questions.

What's new on everyone's done list over the last two weeks?
What's on everyone's to-do list for the next two weeks?
What is the start and completion timings on these to-dos?
Does anyone need any help or want to offer any help?

Like huddles, any time something comes up that requires more conversation or work, it's scheduled by those who will have these conversations. No work is done during sprints.

Team meetings and emails: 9 Don'ts and Do's

Many teams have an unquestioned belief in the necessity and value of team meetings and emails. They believe these have magical abilities to coordinate work.

Actually, more than anything else, they waste time, slow things down, fragment efforts, and prevent alignment and sync. They are tools that were never designed to keep teams aligned and in sync.

That's why we see teams overwhelmed by meetings and emails as they struggle to stay coordinated, aligned, and in sync.

To make things even worse, because they don't know better, they have more meetings and do more emails to try to fix the very disconnects and delays meetings and emails create. This is a costly and unnecessary downward spiral.

Here are 9 rules of thumb to escape and prevent this spiral.

1. Don't have standing team meetings. Especially don't use team meetings for one-on-one updates, reports, or conversations. Use your tech tools. Have team meetings when and for how long they are absolutely needed. Get more done in team work sessions that

produce actual deliverables through collaborative action.

2. Don't have meetings and emails to report on and talk about what can be posted and read on group texts. Create agreements on how group text like Slack and Teams can do a better job of real-time and asynchronous information, questions, and resolution flow.

3. Don't use email as a team. Use it with people outside the team. Use group text, workflow boards, and whiteboards to share work, questions, answers, asks, offers, and ideas.

4. Don't have a video meeting when it can just be a phone call. Meetings with whiteboards work well by phone especially any time we are generating ideas and organizing priorities and work together.

5. Don't have a whole group do the work a small group could do. Excuse anyone from a conversation they don't need to have. Never have people wasting time as passive bystanders to other people's conversations. Have small groups start and complete work for the team.

6. Don't have topic-based agendas. These are the root cause of disengagement, dominating, disappearing, digression, disconnects, and distractions. Organize meetings by questions instead. Any topic can be turned into one or more focusing and engaging questions.

7. Don't have one person lead all meetings. There are multiple engagement and development benefits to having facilitation rotated through the team.

8. Don't have push-based reports outs. These are where individuals push updates out to the team based on what they want people to know and assume they want to know. Use pull-based updates where people with information answer questions from the team and fill in important things that questions didn't address.

9. Don't use meetings and emails as substitutes for huddles. Use huddles as ways to reduce and eliminate time-wasting meetings and team emails. Experiment with different huddle tempos and structures.

Generativity

Design thinking

Teams design any number of things. They design products, services, solutions, experiences, processes, systems, structures, and approaches.

When something works well, it's because it's well designed for its use and use context conditions. When something doesn't work well, it's because it wasn't well designed. Things work exactly as they are designed to work.

When teams haven't yet learned design thinking they confuse design with discussion, debate, and voting. Design thinking is the opposite.

Design thinking has three iterative components: empathy, creativity, and prototyping.

Everything designed has users. These are people who depend on the design to solve for a problem they have. Design thinking is sometimes referred to as human-centered design because it works from empathy.

Empathy is the opposite of assumptions. In empathy, we study the user's experience, emotions, and world relative to the problems we're solving for.

What are the problems we are solving for?
Who are the users, the people with these problems?
How many different kinds of users do we know about and could there be?
In the problem context of our focus what do they experience, how, and why?

We use observations, interviews, and research to answer our questions. The key is to get direct and detailed examples of what users actually experience in the problem context, particularly everything they feel, do, and try doing along the way.

As empathy progresses, we move into creativity. In creativity, we generate as many possible approaches as we can, working from our empathy learnings.

What are all the elements, variables, features, and functions of the problem?
What could be different variations on these?
What would be entirely different approaches to the problem?

We work from the principle that when it comes to ideas, quantity leads to quality. The more apparently good and bad ideas the better. We can enrich our ideas by generating all the questions we can think of relative to possible approaches.

In prototyping, we test rough versions of promising approaches to learn how users experience each. We use this learning to do quick multiple iterations until we have an approach worthy of commitment and investment.

What would minimal viable products look like?
What are we learning from users in each test iteration?
How could we use our learning cycles to improve on our approach?

The power of prototyping is that it supports us to fail fast, fail well, and fail often.

We can apply design thinking to anything we want to create, develop, or implement.

Designing the experience of people we support

We are interested not only in the quality and value of our deliverables to those who depend on us for these, but we are also equally interested in the quality and value of their experience with us.

This is because our relationships with them are core to our success and growth as a team and organization.

A few questions support the design of optimal experiences with us.

What are all the points of contact people experience with us? When do they interact with anyone on our team, how, and why?
What are all the emotions they feel at each point? What do we know for sure and what should we look into and confirm?
What are the little things for us that are the big things for them (moments of truth)?
Where could things get bottlenecked, delayed, slowed down, confusing, or frustrating for them?
How could we get more in sync around these for a better experience?
What would it take to turn any negatives into positives? What could we experiment with to make their experience more consistently high value and positively memorable and recommendable?

We then engage the team in answering these questions and engage design thinking for the best experience model possible. We do this on a regular basis.

Growing ideas

To say ideas are living things is accuracy, not a metaphor. Simply through language, teams can nurture and negate promising ideas. They grow new ideas that work by creating the language conditions for them.

These are the 5 language idea nutrients: like, more, add, when, and both-and. We invite each with questions.

Like: *What do you like about this idea?*

Every idea has some benefit, some advantage, some upside. We don't have to like all of it. We don't have to agree with it completely. We simply acknowledge its potential value.

When we declare what we like about an idea, people with the idea feel heard. When people feel heard they no longer feel the urgency to defend and protect it. New options become possible.

We become open to learning about it, from it, and beyond it. Ideas grow best when people feel welcome to voice their ideas without self-editing and self-filtering. We are more generative together when we are more relaxed together.

New ideas do not grow when we feel we have to be on the defensive. We put each other on the defensive when our first reaction to any idea is questioning, pushing back, attacking its validity, or pointing out obvious deficiencies and risks.

The parts of our brain involved in creativity, passion, and clear decision making shut down when we go into negative judgment mode.

When we say what we like about an idea, we can learn more from and about it. We no longer have to reject or accept it. We allow it to inspire new perspectives.

When we identify anything we like about an idea, what we like gives shape to other possibilities. We build on what we like. Like is the foundation for new differences to consider. We can grow an idea we like in some way. We can start to think of other alternatives and variations.

It's important to be specific. We name all the things we like about an idea and why those matters. We name all likable features, functions, and potential benefits and impacts.

More: *So can you tell me more about this idea?*

Every idea raises questions. We want to know about who, what, when, where, how, why. We want to know if and what about.

Curiosity is the opposite of judgment. It is a space of presence. Ideas grow in the present, not in the past or future.

More questions lead to better questions. There are better questions but we can't judge any question until we see what it leads to. It's just important that we don't reject questions. Each question leads to better questions.

People many times have more in mind than they initially express. The more details we get, the more we can help ideas grow. The more we detail what an idea could be like, the more clearly we become on the potentials of the idea. This is why it's important to ask what else people can tell us about any idea.

Add: *And what could we add to make this idea stronger?*

We can add another element, feature, or dimension. We can add a twist or variation. We can add another way to make it more functional, realistic, or feasible in our use context.

The addition can be small or large. It can be within or beyond our scope of resources and capabilities.

We think of minimal viable products: *What could be the simplest version, given our current resources and capabilities, that could allow us to try it, experiment with it, and prototype it?*

One way to find new additions is to look into and consider similar functional contexts. Every functional analogy will offer a new way of thinking about how to strengthen an idea.

We can research how nature solves this kind of problem. We can research into approaches to problems with similar features and dynamics of our problem of focus.

When: *When could this idea happen, given what needs to come before?*

With ideas, as in life, timing is everything.

Many times the difference between a good idea and a less good idea is timing. An idea is good if it is useful. It is useful when its time is right. An idea that appears to be good but is ahead of or behind its time is not useful.

Having a sense of timing gets us considering what else if anything needs to occur for this idea to work. We might discover that we need to put many new things in place in order for a potentially good idea to work.

Asking what would need to happen before this illuminates prerequisites. Many ideas emerge before their time. They are potentially good and we're not ready for them. Other things have to happen first. Knowing what would have to happen first makes any idea more feasible, attractive, and possible.

We cannot always know exactly when an idea can become reality. We can make estimates that split the difference between our most optimistic and pessimistic scenarios.

We can identify all the precedent ideas that might need to happen first. The more complex and novel an idea, the more previous steps it will require.

Because an idea can't work today doesn't guarantee it also won't in the future. The idea for a laptop before the typewriter era would have been labeled unworkable, but possible once a typewriter and a thousand other ideas would come to fruition first.

Every big new idea stands on the shoulders of countless previous ideas. It's an interesting exercise to take any innovation today and research or at least consider all the innovations back to the discovery of fire that would have had to happen just to make even one of these an affordable, effective reality today.

Both-and: *How else could we optimize the advantages and minimize the disadvantages of this idea?*

Every idea has downsides. Downsides are costs, issues, and problems. They are not necessarily fatal. They are not reasons to abandon the essential goodness of the idea.

They are problems and puzzles to research and solve. They are calls for prototyping alternatives and variations.

Ideas grow best when we name the disadvantages we can see to our own ideas. This opens the space for others to feel free to do the same. This allows us to be realistic together.

The else question is particularly useful when we're at the crossroads of two either-or ideas, such as whether we should give people more freedom or more structure.

Both sides of polarities have upsides and downsides. We generate ideas on how we can make the upsides even more possible and how we can make the downsides even less possible.

We also consider else in the inclusion of other people who can bring new perspectives, questions, alternatives, learning, and experience.

The more diversity of thinking in a group, the more fertile the ground for growing ideas. When we invite people into growing ideas, we make it clear we're asking them to engage the 5 nutrients in the process. Inviting ideas

You can inadvertently limit the generation of ideas by personalizing your own ideas. This is saying things like My idea is… or I think that… or I would argue that…

Especially when your team defers to you with respect to your position, attributing personal ownership to ideas puts people in a position of being loyal or disloyal to your idea instead of feeling free to consider and create variations and alternatives.

In contrast, you can invite ideas by framing yours as One idea is…; One way could be…; One hope is…; One concern and question is… These open the door to more ideas which is important because more ideas lead to better ideas.

The more we understand this principle the more we see our offerings as sparks, seeds, and springboards rather than dares for disagreement, disruption, or disloyalty.

It is also good practice when wanting to engage varieties of ideas to avoid the ambiguous question: So what do you think? It's more generative to be specific.

What do you like about this idea?
What would you change about it?
What else might work as well or better?
What would be some other ideas that would be less than perfect?
What would be some ideas that differ from the usual way things are done?

These have the power to open creative potentials.

Preparing the soil

In talking about ideas as living things, soil preparation means inviting people to do research on our creative focus.

Who else has been and is working on this problem?
What have they tried and learned?
What new approaches are they testing and investing in?
What's the history of this problem?
What are experts studying and saying about it?

Our learning from these questions creates more fertile soil for the creative process.

Creativity is not about staring at a blank page or canvas in hopes that the inspiration muses will magically appear. It is giving our mind as many stimuli as possible to spark new possibilities, varieties, and variations.

How creativity works

Creative teams know from experience that it takes a variety of conditions for ideas to spark, grow, and mature into successful solutions to problems.

People need time on their own to consider new approaches, variations, and syntheses. They need time together, to create, critique, and move ideas forward.

Gathering people around a whiteboard curated by a recorder in a meeting and then voting is one of the best ways to limit creative potentials on a team.

It is vital that people post their own ideas along with voicing them aloud. It is also productive to have them do rough drawings and depictions of ideas. There is a stronger relationship between our hands and brains than between our mouths and brains.

The instructions are simple: You can post an idea and then speak it out loud or speak it out loud and then post it.

Aside from optimizing creative thinking, it keeps people inviting and engaging rather than dominating or disappearing. It applies to every creative and work session.

Learning

The primacy of learning

As trusted leaders, we want to make it easier for people to learn. Learning makes progress possible.

A lack of progress on anything does not necessarily signal a lack of accountability, motivation, or character.

We work from the principle that people always do what they can given what they know at the time. Change in performance, interaction, or the velocity of progress comes from change in what people know. Learning is the expansion of knowing.

People and teams learn their way into progress in any dimension and domain of their work. Learning is the cornerstone and touchstone of flourishing teams. That's why trust, empathy, and respect are vital. They make learning more possible.

Learning questions

Making learning easier for team members and teams means inviting people to always have active learning questions they're working on.

These can be related to any aspects of their work and development including new and higher levels of skills, knowledge, specialization, interaction, performance, and well-being. They can be learning more about our markets and industry. They can be learning more about any relevant research, expert publications, and macro trends.

Learning questions are *How can I...?* and *How can we...?* questions.

We suggest people keep a prioritized, agile, and shared a list of learning questions. We can convene regular conversations where people share their questions and learning. We do the same, leading by example.

When people are just getting started shaping learning questions, it's helpful to have them get into growth mindsets. A few questions help.

What are some things you have learned, improved on, or mastered during your career so far?
What are examples of how you rebounded from a crisis or setback or overcame a challenge?

Feedforward

Where feedback reflects on the past, feedforward focuses on the future. The more feedforward we do the less feedback is necessary. This minimizes the costs of time and tension.

This is good news for leaders and team members who don't particularly enjoy feedback on either side of giving or receiving.

Feedforward is clarifying doneness for any given assignment. We start with the question: What's your understanding here of what great, good, and not yet is?

Every assignment has users, people who will somehow be impacted by the outcomes of the assignment. Great is something users find excellent. Good is something users find adequate. Not yet is something users don't yet find good.

The idea here is to make sure people have a clear idea of all three levels of doneness for any assignment.

Then we check for understanding. *What about all this makes sense to you? Do you have any questions or concerns?*

We address with them any questions or concerns. If we have any doubts about what to expect we can do one last check: How confident are you feeling right now about doing this at the levels of good or great? When useful, we offer ideas to boost their confidence and ours.

Having unrequested feedback for others

For any number of reasons, we have assessments about people's work they have not requested or invited. These could be people on our team, peers, or leaders above us.

We observe them or something they communicated, did, or produced. We hear about them or something they communicated, did, or produced.

We might not know if what we have to share would be news for them, meaning it's one of their unknowns unknown unknowns. We might also not know if they would be receptive to or interested in our assessments.

So, we ask.

Notice ideas and questions replace feedback because it's true, useful, and less potentially emotionally charged.

What would you like me to do with ideas and questions I have about your work that you're not asking me for?
What do you want others to do with ideas and questions they have?
Are there any kinds of ideas and questions about your work you would like from me and others? What kind, when, and how?

Do you want to create some agreements with me and others on how you can get ideas and questions on your work from them and me?

It is useful to include feedforward in any feedback conversations. It is also good practice to ask for feedforward and feedback insights from people on the team about your own work as a leader.

Wanting unshared feedback

There are many reasons why people would have feedback for you that they don't share.

They didn't enjoy the last time they gave you feedback you asked for or that they gave you unrequested by you. They don't think it's their job to give you feedback you don't request. They think you already know what they have to share and have decided not to do anything differently.

They don't know how to word their feedback in a way they think you will receive it well. They are concerned you might deny or argue with their feedback. They are not optimistic you will act on their feedback. They don't want you to perceive them as critical, negative, or demanding.

Any of these can keep people from sharing feedback you're not explicitly requesting from them. As you build trust with people and ask for feedback they will feel more confident in giving you useful feedback.

Trust starts with our transparency around feedback. This can sound something like: *I'm always in learning mode, so your perspectives and insights are important to me. The kinds of ideas and questions about my work I would find most useful are...*

We can also ask:

Do you feel free to share with me ideas about my work as leader? How so?
Would anything make it easier to do so?
When it comes to my work as leader do you have any questions or ideas for me today?

We have conversations and agreements with others about what, how, and when they would find feedback useful.

Career crafting

Inviting people to talk about their sense of their career is a compelling way to support their potential for learning.

The more people trust us as leaders, the more open they are to talk about the arc and dynamics of their careers parallel to and beyond their work on the team today.

Even with trust, they might only initiate these conversations if they know or think we are interested in their careers and also want to have these conversations.

Their not initiating these conversations tells us nothing. We have to offer and request.

This is one version of an invitation: *I want you to know I'm interested in your sense of your career now and I'm offering to be a sounding board or source of ideas and questions if and when you'd like.*

If they accept the invitation, other questions can shape the dialogue and agreements.

When talking with people about their career paths several options are possible.

There are people who don't think ahead at all. They feel content, stuck, or uneasy crafting a sense of a future because there are too many variables out of their control.

There are those who are interested in always learning, growing, and expanding their career possibilities. They want to keep an eye open to new development and work opportunities.

There are people who want to transition to retirement. Their transition will be more smooth and meaningful with a sense of what they want to do beyond their current work or career.

What each has in common is uncertainty, more unknowns than knowns. A path forward is viable when we leverage unknowns as assets.

This is a four-part iterative, question-based process.

When you think about your future, what are your hopes, concerns, uncertainties, and interests?
What would these look like if you turned them into questions like how can I, should I, what if I, and could I?
What actions could answer any of these questions, actions like research, experiments, learning, conversations, and decisions?
In what order would it make sense to work on these questions and when can you work on them?

What happens is that answers to their questions reveal new questions and possibilities.

They move forward one question at a time. Each new question reveals new options and opportunities. They create a meaningful future one question at a time.

More questions to consider:

Do you have a sense of what you want to be doing after the work you're doing now?
Are there ways you might want to see your work change at some point?
Do you have some options to either you're considering?
Are there any things you'd like to be learning over the next year or two, new skills, or areas of expertise?
Would you like some ideas on these learning interests?

When relevant, we offer help, teaching, or resources for any of their learning questions.

Work crafting

Work crafting is being intentional about the meaning and value of a team member's work. It is another way to support their learning potentials.

We have a social responsibility to make sure people have work they can do well including when they're onboarding or offboarding.

Part of this is making sure work assignments are based on reality rather than assumptions.

Here are assumptions not to operate from:
- If the assignments they're getting seem to relate to their education, training, and work histories, they probably can and want to do this work well
- If they did similar work before, they probably can do this work without additional learning or support
- If they did similar work before, it was probably assessed by the same standards and agreements we have today
- If they inherited certain assignments because of the role they're in, they probably can and want to do this work
- If they are handed assignments because they're the only ones capable or available, they probably can and want to do them
- If they have a job description with this work assigned, it likely means they are capable of and interested in doing it well

We can turn each assumption into a question to determine their actual ability, confidence, and willingness to do any assignment.

When someone starts showing a pattern of work not done well, we can ask if they still want to do it. It's a fair and respectful predictive question. If they do, we can explore learning supports from us or others.

If they don't we can explore if anyone else can take it, share it, or rotate it. We then ask: Is there anything else they would want to take on?

If nothing is possible, we just need to be honest about this: *This needs to be done and you are the only one who can do this. I don't have another option except to ask you. Is there anything I can do to make doing this easier?*

Sometimes we get to the question of how long we allow someone to have assignments they're struggling to do well. We have to decide if someone is in an explicit learning process focused on any assignments at risk and if they're making progress and at what rate.

We have to decide when the costs of their slow learning velocity no longer warrant them continuing to get these assignments or continue as a member of the team.

At some point, we might have to ask some direct clarifying questions like: *Do you feel confident you can be a strong contributor to the team? What does that mean to you? Are you clear about what it means to no longer be a member of the team?*

These are respectful questions the precede requesting work changes.

As soon as we see someone's membership on the team at risk, we declare this to them and make it clear as leader, for the team's sake, we must search for someone to take their assignments. The idea here the principle of zero surprises.

Anytime they do something well, we comment on it. Anytime they fall short, we ask: *Did you think you would fall short here? What are you learning? Who can help you do this learning?*

We keep supporting their learning until their last day with the team. That is our work as a trusted leader.

We can even say to them: *Your being or not being a member of the team is entirely your responsibility. It's up to you to be a member of the team or not. I just want to make it easier for you to take responsibility for this and learn all you can while you're a team member. I will not support your having work you cannot learn to do well.* We always bring everything back to learning.

We are prepared for people to succeed or fail at this point. Our work as a trusted leader is to keep our language with them consistently clear, humble, empathetic, encouraging, and realistic as well as to use and invite as many language actions as possible.

That's our scope of responsibility.

Consequences

People perform and interact differently when they know the natural consequences of their actions and interactions.

Natural consequences include the outcomes, impacts, costs, and perceptions that result from what people do and communicate. They give shape to assessments, offers, proposals, and requests.

Each of us is capable of creating all manner of unseen and unknown consequences of what we do, say, and ask. When we aren't sure if someone knows the natural consequences of their actions, we ask.

When you are on time with... What do you imagine happens as a result?
When you are late with...what do you imagine happens as a result?

If they need help thinking through this, ask: *Is it possible that...?* and offer possibilities.

We can begin with areas we know they're doing well. Where they have assumptions and other unknowns, we work with them to find ways to identify these consequences.

We can then move onto more challenging areas where they have little or no accurate and up to date insights.

We're not giving them the unkind language of anonymous assessment. We want to create an environment where people feel invited and valued for requesting, offering, and sharing awareness of consequences. This takes work with the whole team if they are not accustomed to it.

Imposed consequences are things like mandating time off and giving them negative performance review scores.

Even when these must occur they do not substitute for awareness of natural consequences. Imposed consequences have no power to help people become more conscious of their natural consequences.

If people become anxious or angry with imposed consequences, they could go into defensiveness and even denial of their failure, making fixed mindsets possible.

People have self-trust, pride in work, and a growth mindset when they are aware of natural consequences.

The promises of extrinsic positive incentives and threats of extrinsic negative punishments can artificially propel people into temporary and disingenuous compliance.

We bring natural consequences to someone's attention when we describe them in detail. *When you're late on this, your teammates have to scramble and sometimes disappoint those who depend on us. It puts them behind on other work and they might have to experience preventable family tensions because they have to distress family schedules to catch up.*

This helps people become more aware of the actual impacts and implications of their actions and communications. The call for holding people accountable often comes up when we have yet to help people become more consequence conscious.

Everyone has different levels of attention beyond themselves. The larger the scope of attention the more potential people have for positive impacts including those they never directly observe.

Even getting them to imagine natural consequences influences their performance and interactions. *When you do that, it makes it more likely for people to feel...and as a result...*

Most importantly we do this with positive situations. *When you let people know you're going to be late on something, you give them the option to shift their focus or help you out if they can, so that's better for them than guessing. Any moments of success can be the focus of natural consequences awareness.*

Failure

At some point, it is useful to talk to people about failure. It can or not be associated with an event. We suggest there is good failure and bad failure.

Good failure is failure in learning, experiments, and prototyping. The key in each is to fail fast, fail well, and fail often.

Bad failure is failing from mistakes and errors. Mistakes are incorrect actions, actions that don't deliver what's defined as great or good. It's something that's not useful or helpful. Errors are incorrect assumptions, assumptions that are not aligned with reality.

When we're talking with someone about a possible future failure they might be anxious about, we can talk about what good and bad failure might look like then.

When talking about a past failure, we can still talk about what good and bad failure could have looked like. *What could good and bad failure look like in this kind of situation?*

This positions good failure as a viable source of new ideas, insights, perspectives, questions, and options going forward.

Fear of failure can keep people from honest communication, making commitments, starting things, completing things, trying or learning new things, and taking on new assignments.

The key to all this is high-value language. This spells out exactly what kinds of flaws, errors, gaffes, mistakes, and defects are ultimately unacceptable. When progress is defined, we agree on the decreasing patterns of failure expected and accepted.

A few questions work:

What kinds of failure would be natural here?
What kinds would be unacceptable?
What could we learn from failing fast, well, and often?

Any instances of an individual team member or team failures, setbacks, and disappointments are prime opportunities for the question: What are we learning here from this that we can take forward? Keep the focus entirely on future applications especially when people waste time in unkind and disrespectful blame or defensiveness.

Peer to peer teaching

Having people teach each other anything has three benefits.

The teacher improves in what they're teaching. Learning is more accessible and accelerated. The relationship between them strengthens which strengthens the overall bonds within the team.

Having the learner video the teaching makes it available for them and others later. Everything taught is optimally on video. Having the teacher video the learner accelerates the learner's progress and success and again becomes archived resources for others.

The advantage of peer over expert teaching is that peers can have the language closer to the learner's natural language for learning.

They could also be more empathetic than an expert or high-level performer. This facilitates learning velocity and use. Pairing people on assignments is the most natural way for learning sharing.

Storytelling

Storytelling is the oldest human teaching tradition. Only in recent human history do people think learning could happen without storytelling.

As trusted leaders, we live, share, and invite stories. We use stories to engage, inspire, teach, and connect. Stories have a unique power in building trust. The showing in stories is the opposite of telling in lectures.

Stories have four simple language structures: unresolved uncertainties, interest-generating references, relatable emotions, and uncertainty resolutions.

Unresolved certainty is a problem, challenge, tension, question that listeners hope one of the characters resolves. Interest-generating references are the ways the unfolding story teases us with hints of unseen influences and unpredictable twists and turns.

Relatable emotions are explicit and implied emotions the characters are experiencing in the story. The more the better.

Uncertainty resolution is the story conclusion that in some ways answers the curiosity evoked in the opening phases of the story.

Stories have power when there are a range and variety of positive and negative language tone and high and low language value. The more variety the stronger the story is and the more listeners engage in the story and bond with the storyteller.

Stories well-told have richer language because we are showing not telling what characters are doing and experiencing, and with whatever they do, we get an inside look into their minds and hearts along the way.

Keep a list of stories you can use in any situation. These can be your own stories as well as stories of others

Practice stories and get feedback from others as well. Invite stories among team members for any occasion. Do research on storytelling and spend time with people who are good storytellers.

Leaders of leaders

When we are leaders supporting other leaders, we give attention to how they and their teams are doing. Our work is to support their success as leaders through continuous learning.

We regularly check in on where things are going well and, most importantly, why.

What's going well on your team?
Why do you think these things are going well? How does your team describe the why of their progress and success?

We offer additional insights and questions. We want to build the confidence these leaders have in themselves and their teams.

We keep up with their work with their team.

Where do you find yourself spending most of your time?
What are you currently working on to make things easier for people you support?
What are you learning so far?

If they are struggling with any team members, we leave that work up to them, only intervening when they request it. In the meantime, we work with them on their leadership language.

We want to support their being proactive.

What's ahead for you that you're particularly paying attention to?
Are there any conversations you think you need to be inviting or convening?

On a regular basis, we also check in on their learning questions.

What learning questions are you working on now?
What feedback is telling you where you are on these?
Are there any ideas you would like from me?

Just as we want them to make life easier for their teams we stay transparent about and engaged in making life easier for them.

Personas

Persona mindsets

Teams are commonly populated by a variety of personas. A persona is a mindset. Each different mindset shapes ways of acting, interacting, communicating, and learning. Any can show up in any generation. Here are a dozen examples.

Struggling

People with struggling mindsets believe work is inevitably challenging. This can be a more chronic, reoccurring, or recent belief.

They might appear overwhelmed, frazzled, and disorganized. What's clear is that we and they don't yet have a shared sense of how they understand their work.

What are your current tasks, decisions, and communications?
What's your understanding of the standards for each?
What levels are you at for each?
What learning questions are you working on?

If they miss anything, we fill in the gaps with clarifications. Then we get into their sense of struggle.

When do you feel most overwhelmed, frustrated, lost, or behind?
What isn't easy for you?

Then we focus forward.

What might progress look like in these areas?
When is it OK and not OK to fail?
When is it OK and not OK to ask for help?

We clarify what for them is inaccurately understood or unclear. Then, the most important aspect here is to support their being well organized.

What are your systems and routines for staying organized?

We get a detailed sense of what they do and don't do and ask if they want any ideas, especially sharing with them our own favorite ways to stay organized. The key is them experimenting with as many ways as it takes for progress.

We share our intention: *I want you to feel confident in your ability to do your work well without it being harder than it needs to be.*

These are helpful conversations particularly for people who have not had them before with trusted leaders or even friends and partners.

Inconsolables

People with an inconsolables mindset believe that if we talk about problems enough they will get solved. This mindset fosters a sense that nothing ever seems good enough. They usually don't keep it to themselves. It can be a minor or major energy-suck for others on the team.

We begin by getting them to enumerate their list of grievances. *What bothers you most in your work?*

When it appears they named everything they can, we conclude with: *Is this everything or is there anything else?* We want them to become aware that, although their complaining can be endless, their list is finite.

We get them clear on the boundaries of their agency: *Do you feel like you have any influence or control over these?* Then ask: *What do you think you do have direct control and influence over?* This helps them move from helplessness to a sense of agency and limits.

Then we can further explore where they could improve their work. *When do you feel most and least productive?* We can problem-solve with them any areas where they feel least productive.

One more way to shift them into agency is helping them get more clear on their impact: *Do you think you get enough useful feedback from me and the team?*

If they don't: *Is there anything else that would be useful to you?*

We check on where learning might be possible. *What do you think your learning questions could be?* We ask if they want some ideas. We offer learning support and make any agreements with them that make sense.

We conclude with getting them more clear on their value to the team: *What's your sense of how important your work is to the team?* If they are clueless or unclear, we share our perspectives.

One foot out the door

People with one foot out the door mindset believe their success has come down to staying below the radar and out of trouble.

It is our assessment that they are at risk for separation from the team. They are showing little to no progress, or regress. We are not sure they even know the reality of this risk.

We have coached them on several aspects of their work. They might have a serious lack of motivation for the work, disconnection from the team and its why, or both. Now it's time for some ultimate conversations.

We start with the big picture. *What do you think it means to be a member of this team?* We fill in gaps and make any clarifications we need to so their picture is accurate and complete.

Then we respectfully check for commitment. *Do you still want to be a member of this team?* We will get a refusal, an unclear or qualified commitment, or a clear commitment.

We make commitments. *It's my work to do whatever I can to help you succeed here if you commit to continuing on the team. It's also my work to make sure you are clear on what it means to be a member of this team.*

Then we spell out in detail what else they would need to be able and willing to do to be an engaged member of the team. We check on their clarity and commitment levels.

Can you give me your understanding of this?
How confident are you that you could do this
What is your confidence (or unconfidence) based on?
Is there anything I can do to support your confidence and success?

As usual, we check in on them regularly and use our most respectful, empathetic, and trusted leadership language. It's all we can do.

Eye on the door

People with an eye on the door mindset believe that all they need at this point is to cruise.

We declare our intentions. *You have been and continue to be a valued member of the team. I want especially the younger team members to gain as much of your experience, expertise, and wisdom you're willing to share. I want you to be able to reflect backward and forward on your time with the team and the team's future.*

Start with reflection on the past.

What would you say were your best and most challenging times with the team?
What do you think you learned in your experience with the team?

What do you think the team learned in the time you were with the team?

Then focus on the future.

What would you like to see possible for the team beyond your tenure with them?
How would you most like to see younger team members grow and develop?
Are any of these areas of strength for you?
Would you be willing to spend time sharing what you have?

Finally, outline some possible commitments and agreements.

Do you think succession conversations would be productive now? If so, how? If not, why not?
Are there any things you'd like to learn, contribute, or accomplish before you leave the team and if so how could these become possible?
Would you want to come back in any capacity and if so how could we make this more possible now?

Celebrate with them any and all of their contributions to the team. Encourage team members to engage and appreciate them when possible.

The entitled class

People with an entitled mindset believe their success is being served by others. For any number of reasons, they are used to being served and getting their way. They have moments of being self-absorbed and self-promoting. They might also experience little honest interest in the needs or struggles of others.

We want to shift their focus to the team and their place in it.

What do you think the team is doing well?
Where do you think it's struggling at all?
What do you think our team is and isn't capable of?
What do you base this on?

We complete any incomplete picture they offer and clarify any assumption errors. Then we invite them to think about others who depend on their contributions.

Who depends on you and who do you most impact?
What do you want their experience to be?
How could you make sure they have this experience?

Finally, we get them into a growth mindset.

What are your current learning questions?
What do you think you want to or could get better at?
How could you answer these learning questions?

Who will benefit from you doing this learning and how will they benefit? How will you benefit?
What can you do to make this learning happen?

Make sure they realize any gaps in their understanding of performance and interaction standards and form learning questions where indicated.

Make your intention clear: *I want people to be able to depend on you as the strong contributor I think you are and can be.*

Guardians of the status quo

People with a guardians of the status quo mindset believe the way it is is good enough. They consider not rocking the boat virtuous and necessary for self-survival.

They might be averse to risk, change, and learning because of a significant intolerance to failure. They might have a fixed mindset, believing they are not capable of learning more than they already know. They might have the arrogance of assuming there is nothing else for them to know.

They might resist anything new because doing so would mean they were wrong in compliance with the old ways. They might be afraid that if they say yes to anything more, even more will be asked of them. A change in the status quo might mean the loss of position, power, control, or protection from consequences.

Sometimes defending the status quo is a long-term pattern that extends into most or much of their personal lives.

There is also an interesting dynamic where people get used to the status quo because their organizations resist change, creating the defensive comfort zones that exist today.

We start by opening the possibility that change is inevitable.

What do you think could never change about our team, its work, the organization?
Why do you think so?
Are there any reasons why anything could or would change?

We offer our insights that align with or counter what we hear. Then we continue to normalize the idea, validity, and benefits of change:

Have you seen any ways our team and the organization have gotten any faster, better, or easier in the past couple of years?
Do you think the team learned from its successes and failures? What are examples?
What benefits did these bring about?

Complete the picture with any facts, examples, anecdotes, and stories.

Engage them in the consideration of change: *Is there anything about your work and the team's work you'd like to be easier, better, or faster?*

Add any suggestions and ask if they'd be willing to be a part of any relevant experiments.

Finally, directly address failure-aversion. *What's your understanding of when failure is expected and good in our work, and when it isn't?*

Complete and clarify their understanding and encourage good failure.

We invite these conversations with the whole team if the dominant vibe is a guardian of the status quo mindset.

Hyper-achievers

People with a hyper-achievers mindset believe they are never getting enough done or they're never perfect enough.

Their perfectionism emanates from dread of failure. Failure is the vast and treacherous gap between good and perfect. Even as the team benefits in the short term they drive themselves in unsustainable ways.

We can begin by sharing our intentions: *I want you to work in a sustainable way and not burn yourself out. You are a valued and valuable member of the team and the team needs you.*

Then we invite realistic expectations: *What do you consider your fair share of contribution to the team?*

We can affirm and challenge what we can. A follow-up question could be: *What are your beliefs about what success is for you? Could anything else be true?*

We want to invite them to question unquestioned unrealistic beliefs that lead to them being hard on themselves. We want to make sure they are clear on what we consider success to be for them.

We also want to make it easier for them to ask for help. *When do and don't you feel OK with asking for help?* We offer ideas they don't have.

Find out if they have confidence in any team members relative to any of their specific assignments. *Are there people who you think could learn to be able to do anything you do?*

They might not accurately assess the performance, learning, or willingness potential of others. For people we consider possible we ask: *What do you think about...?*

We can offer to invite a conversation with them and eligible others to explore assignment handoffs, pairing, rotations, and learning. Then we explore other possibilities of relief.

Is there anything taking longer than you think it should? This could be a call for their asking for help or their learning.

Two other areas might be useful. *Do you ever feel free to say no or later to anything? How many breaks do you take, for how long, what do they involve?*

We share our intention here: *I want you to do your fair share of work and be a sustainable member of the team.*

Newbies

People with a newbies mindset believe they will eventually get their bearings and feel like a fully contributing team member.

They are new to the team, the organization, or both. A few onboarding design questions are useful.
We can start with the question: *What will onboarding doneness look like?* We outline with them an agile onboarding approach. We can also invite members of the team to this.

What do we want them to be able to feel, know, and do in the next 6 weeks?
What can we and others do to make these possible?
How can everyone on the team be engaged in this support?

We revisit these questions every 6 weeks with the new team member and the team.

In our check-ins with new people, we ask any or all of these:

Where do you feel most and least confident in your work?
Do you know who to go to and for what?
What is your sense of the best use of your time in the next 2 weeks?
Is anything puzzling, confusing, or frustrating so far?
Do you ever find yourself waiting for anything or anyone? And if so, when and why?

We create any kinds of useful solutions, approaches, checklists, connections, and agreements.

Soloists

People with soloist mindsets believe they do their best work alone.

They can be friendly and receptive to helping and working with others when indicated. They live by the idea that good fences make good neighbors.

Because self-reliance is a strength, they don't as a rule ask for help or complain when they struggle.

Checking in on them on a regular basis is a good idea. *How's it going? How are you doing on your assignments?*

It's also a good idea to share our intention with them, perhaps opening the conversation with a question: *Do you feel comfortable letting me know when you might get stuck or overwhelmed?*

If not, we can make our intention for that clear: *I don't care how busy I might seem, I want you to let me offer support when it would possibly be helpful.*

We can also check to see if they feel comfortable asking others for help, and encouraging them to make agreements with others on the team to share help.

Careerists

People with a career-driven mindset believe the work they have today is one career stepping stone in more to come.

We check to see if they are willing to have a career conversation with us. *Would you be comfortable and interested in sharing your career wishes and aspirations?*

If they decline our offer: *If you ever would like to I would be very happy to have a conversation. The more I understand where you're heading the more I can support you being prepared for it. Understand that these would be confidential conversations unless there are specific things you would want to share with specific others.*

If they agree to a conversation:

How would you describe your career interests today? Have they shifted, how, and why?
Are there parts of your work today that are relevant to these?
Is there work you would like to take on or learn that could be relevant to these?
Are you doing anything outside of work to move forward?
Are there any ways I could support your moving forward?
Are there people on the team who could support you or learn from you?

We do what we can to offer and commit to support and check in on a regular basis.

I want your work to contribute value to those we support, the team, and your career. I want to support your career path as long as you're part of the team. I want you to also be a source of support to the learning of others on the team.

Likables

People with likable mindsets believe being liked gives them the best possible advantage in their work and beyond. They are people others just like because they are friendly, dependable, helpful, respectful, and easy to work with.

Not only are they not perfect, but their sense of humility also inspires them to continuously explore, learn, and expand their perspective.

In conflicts, disagreements, and tensions, they listen for understanding and voice a clear bias for win-win and both-and over win-lose and either-or. People trust them and feel comfortable asking them for help and being a listening ear.

Like soloists, it might not always be clear when they need support or different engagement opportunities.

We begin with our intention: *I want to make sure you have work that you want to do. You are valuable to the team and I don't want to miss opportunities to support your success and well-being.*

One question then is: *So, how happy are you with your mix of assignments? Is there anything different you'd like to take on or learn to take on?*

These are often people with growth mindsets who get significant meaning out of doing and learning new things. We can make this easier for them.

Entrepreneurs

People with entrepreneurial mindsets believe change is good. They have a passion for solving problems.

They like creating change and engaging others in it. They are change agents, early adopters, and change champions. They are keen on the growth and innovation potentials and aspirations of the team and organization.

If they cannot initiate or participate in change they become frustrated with the status quo and are at risk of disengaging from the team.

Create with them a shared sense of where change opportunities exist now or could exist: *Where do you think we have opportunities to create and adapt to change? Are there problems we should be solving for that we are not yet?*

If they are not yet engaged in an existing change effort we ask:

Do you see yourself being a part of making this change happen?
Are there any ways you would also like to help make this change happen?
Are there any experiments you think we could be doing that we aren't yet?
Are there any ways I can support you in that?

We offer whatever ideas and support we can and check-in regularly. We can also explore where and how they can engage others in any change effort.

Who else do you think is and could be ready for change?
How could you be a connector and storyteller with these people and groups?

We let them know we appreciate their efforts in change and describe the difference we think they are making and can make.

The art of language

Make your leadership language an art. Keep exploring and experimenting with different ways to say and ask things.

Share your leadership language learning questions and learning with trusted friends and colleagues. Build a richly diverse vocabulary.

Keep a journal or notebook of what particularly works and clearly doesn't. Make the Thesaurus your friend and visit with it often. Make your own ear and heart your greatest tools to test and prototype new language.

Certainly, make yours all the language examples throughout the book. Translate anything into your own words that stay true to the intention of impact and attention to respect.

Listening

The power of listening

Feeling heard makes it easier for people to feel respected, valued, and engaged.

When people feel these, they are more open to considering what we and others declare, suggest, offer, and request. They are more likely to make agreements and commitments. They are more eager to learn. They are more honest and empathetic with themselves and others.

When people don't feel understood they shut down. They resist what we and others have to say and ask. They are more likely to resist responsibility. They don't feel free to be honest.

When we show up with integrity in our listening we make it easier for them to listen. People feel respected and interact with us as trusted leaders. It makes our work easier as well.

What trusted listening is not

It's not interrupting, interpreting, or intervening.

We let people talk even and especially when we feel impatient. We test any assumptions we have about what they say and ask. We seek more to understand than to lecture or solve.

It is not the unresponsive absence of speaking. Listening is a language. Feeling understood, respected, and valued happens because of the language we use when listening.

It's not using the time others speak to formulate our reactions or next moves. It's not assuming that everything we hear is all someone knows. It's being far more curious than assumptive.

It's frequently showing the sights and sounds of understanding and empathetic emotions.

When people don't feel heard

Interrupting occurs in myriad forms. We talk over people. We finish their statements. We disregard their questions with interjections. We look away at screens or redirect the conversation to others.

Interpreting suggests or insists we know what someone knows, thinks, or feels before they explicitly share it. *You must be feeling...* and *It sounds like you are...* are interpretations. In both people feel not heard and not understood because we are using our language not theirs.

We express curiosity instead: *Can you tell me more about...?*

Intervening is issuing unsolicited advice and solutions. When we offer ideas and questions it has the language and tone of offers, not impositions and it's once we feel confident people feel heard.

What we offer often works for people because our listening allows us the luxury of having an accurate picture of the realities they operate from and within.

Emotions

As trusted leaders, our prime interest in listening is listening to how people feel. People trust those who take the time to listen well to how they feel.

According to current brain science, emotions don't happen to us, they happen by us. They are not triggered by situations; they are constructed by our brain.

Emotions occur as our brain puts words to feelings to make sense of our moment to moment experience. Feelings are the pleasant and unpleasant physical sensations we experience in any moment. The continuum of pleasant to unpleasant is called affect.

Emotions are felt words like happy and crappy. Emotions don't exist until we put words to feelings. We create them through words.

Along with affect the other characteristic of feelings and emotions is volume. Volume is felt intensity. Pleasant or unpleasant can be more high intensity loud or low intensity quiet. Feeling awesome can be loud or quiet, just as feeling awful can.

The fewer words we use to describe our experience the louder our emotions. The more words we use, the quieter our emotions.

That's what happens when someone listens to us when we're upset As we put more words to our feelings our emotions become progressively quieter precisely because our language becomes more granular, nuanced, and situation-specific.

When our emotions are quieter we have more space for others. We get stuck in louder emotions with fewer words. We get stuck in actions that accompany stuck emotions. When we create space for different emotions we create space for different actions.

We cannot have unconscious emotions we're not aware of because we create them with our words. We can however have the sensations of feelings we haven't yet put words to.

We can have feelings without emotions. We can feel good or bad and not put words to them. When we do put words to them they can shift in affect, volume, or both.

Because emotions are felt words like love and hate any difference in our words actually creates a difference in our emotions.

The granular, situation-specific emotion of the feeling when our fingers search for one last chip in a bag only to find it empty is a different emotion than the generic feeling of sad.

The ability to create quieter and different emotions is the heart of emotional well-being. Emotional well-being is at the heart of doing and being our best in all aspects of our life.

As we listen and offer people more words for their emotional experience than they might have we make it more possible for them to have quieter and therefore other emotions.

We also make this easier when we simply validate that their current emotions make sense given what they know.

In listening well we co-create their emotions and emotional well-being with them. As a result, we make different actions possible as well.

Listening is the greatest gift we give anyone. It is why the language of trusted leadership has the ability to make things easier for people.

Use their words, rhythm, and name

Everyone uses their own language. When we incorporate their language into ours they feel heard.

We listen for their metaphors. People use metaphors about every two dozen spoken words. Metaphors are categories of similarity.

Some examples are: *This project is a beast; I'm burning the candle at both ends; I can see the end of the tunnel; I feel like I'm at a crossroads; It's weighing on me; Hearing the deadline moved back was music to my ears.*

They are emotional trigger words. Using the exact language others use validates the truth of their experience. We reference beasts, candles, tunnels, crossroads, weights, and music. They feel understood. This is using clean language.

When someone talks at roughly the rate of our talking rhythm we feel a subtle resonance that makes trust more possible.

Hearing one's name has the unique power of feeling respected. We can use their name as occasional punctuation, as *You know* (their name)... and *So,* (their name)... Nothing has the power to capture our attention like the sound of our name.

Lectures, threats, and warnings (Oh, my!)

As much as we are tempted, we don't remind and lecture people about what they already know. They don't feel heard.

We also don't impose obvious or thinly disguised threats or warnings. No one feels understood from these.

Telling people what to think is the opposite of making it easier for them to consider other ideas, other perspectives, and questions.

New questions others have not yet considered allow them to be feel heard and invited to consider and feel differently. They invite people to show up differently.

Micro-yeses

We know someone feels heard when they accept the language we use to describe what we hear them saying and asking.

It's not necessary to repeat them verbatim, in fact, it's better to not. Optimally, we use our words to show alignment with their experience.

We ask Is this accurate? after we describe what we hear as a simple way to check for understanding. An alternative includes: Is what you're saying...? Saying could also be thinking, feeling, wanting, wondering, concerned about, and hoping for.

The key here is to ask questions that elicit small, micro-yeses. This heightens their experience of being understood. The more yeses the better.

Listen from good questions

Good questions are those that are new for others. They are ones they haven't considered or looked into. They are ones they are unprepared to answer and so have the power to evoke new perspectives and feeling understood.

If the response to our question seems reflexive and canned, it's not a good question. Good questions evoke and provoke new perspectives or considerations, new offers or commitments, new agreements or acceptances.

In listening, good questions have a unique advantage over statements because of their ability to express interest in others. When we are interested in what others have to say and ask they feel heard. They feel trusted and so become more open to trust.

There is one good question that is perhaps the most useful because it can apply to any situation we encounter: *What else is possible here?*

The question is powerful because it helps shift people immediately from confusion to clarity, from uncertainty to action, from a sense of struggle to agency.

It is the ultimate question in the listening of trusted leaders. It makes a universe of things easier.

On many levels our listening gives our speaking its power. It keeps our language clear, humble, empathetic, encouraging, and respectful.

Epilogue

Our world has never been in the state it is in now. Nothing has prepared us for this. We can only design and learn our way into the world we want to see.

We have an enormous amount of work to do to bring about a world of respect and empathy. Only with a world of respect and empathy will everyone have a chance to flourish.

This is possible when we have trusted leaders committed to the kind of respect and empathy everyone needs to learn, manifest, and share.

It is up to us as leaders to lead in this. To lead is to go first. We must go first. There is no leadership in waiting for others, hoping someone else has the skill and will to be a trusted leader committed to respect and empathy with and for all.

You have the opportunity to become a trusted leader. It is what you have the potential to be and what the world most needs. Everyone will be better for it.

About the author

Jack is co-founder and partner with Cleveland-based Thrive At Work, a firm specializing in planning, leadership, and culture with organizations across industries.

With an undergraduate degree from John Carroll University and a graduate degree from Goddard College, both in psychology, his career began in the late 1970s as a community health therapist trained in American, European, and Japanese methodologies.

In the early 1980s, he pivoted to training and coaching with organizations across 24 industries as well as teaching undergraduate, graduate, and post-doc courses in psychology, management, and entrepreneurship.

Jack is the author of 27 books and sustains a blog launched in August 2002. He lives in the historic neighborhood of Tremont in Cleveland, Ohio.

For more about Jack, his work, and books visit
Nuanceworks.com